ISSUES THAT CONCERN YOU

English Language Learners

Other books in the Issues That Concern You series:

ISSUES THAT CONCERN YOU

English Language Learners

Tamara L. Roleff, *Book Editor*

GREENHAVEN PRESS

A part of Gale, Cengage Learning

GALE
CENGAGE Learning™

Detroit • New York • San Francisco • New Haven, Conn • Waterville, Maine • London

Christine Nasso, Publisher
Elizabeth Des Chenes, Managing Editor

Articles in Greenhaven Press anthologies are often edited for length to meet page
requirements. In addition, original titles of these works are changed to clearly present the main thesis and to explicitly indicate the author's opinion. Every effort is made
to ensure that Greenhaven Press accurately reflects the original intent of the authors.
Every effort has been made to trace the owners of copyrighted material.

Cover image © 2009/Jupiterimages.

LIBRARY OF CONGRESS CATALOGING-IN-PUBLICATION DATA

English language learners / Tamara L. Roleff, book editor.
    p. cm. — (Issues that concern you)
  Includes bibliographical references and index.
  ISBN 978-0-7377-4347-0 (hardcover)
  1. English language—Study and teaching—Foreign speakers.
  I. Roleff, Tamara L., 1959-
  PE1128.A2E486 2009
  428.2'4—dc22
                                                2008046575

Printed in the United States of America
1 2 3 4 5 6 7 13 12 11 10 09

CONTENTS

In Los Angeles, Chinatown is not just a tourist destination filled with Chinese restaurants, tailors, and specialty shops. Chinatown has spread east into the suburbs as Asian immigrants have bought into the American dream of large homes, large yards, expensive cars, and owning their own businesses. Yet many of these immigrants feel as if they have never left Asia. The populations of some suburbs in the valley east of Los Angeles have doubled since the early 1990s, and nearly two-thirds of the residents are Asian. Office and industrial parks are identified by signs in Chinese. Some schools report that close to 60 percent of their students are Asian. Mandarin is more likely to be heard than English in retail stores. Hearing Mandarin everywhere instead of English presents an unlikely problem for some adult immigrants: They have no one with whom they can practice speaking English.

The same is true for immigrants from Mexico. Studies show that Mexican immigrants tend to concentrate in specific areas, stop attending school earlier, and speak less English than other immigrants, although these rates do improve with subsequent generations. And now that Mexican immigrants are starting to settle beyond their traditional gateway homes of California, Texas, Florida, and Illinois, spreading into mainstream America, more Americans are becoming uncomfortably aware of Mexican immigrants and their insular communities.

Some Americans complain that although they are in the United States, it does not feel like it when they enter these immigrant enclaves. Many, if not most, of the signs are in a foreign language, as are most conversations. But these complaints have been heard since the first mass migrations to the United States in the first half of the nineteenth century. The Irish clustered together in Boston, Italians in New York, Germans and Scandinavians in the Midwest. And now, Asians head for the big cities

A California polling place sign lists seven different languages—a testimony to the diversity of California residents.

along both coasts, Mexicans to the South and Southwest, and the Hmong go to Minnesota, Wisconsin, and California.

Ethnic groups and immigrants tend to live near others from the same country both for security and for the sense of familiarity they feel in living near those who speak the same language and share the same customs. However, many Americans argue that immigrants who live in these enclaves delay their assimilation into American society. They are also upset that many immigrants who live in these sheltered communities do not learn English.

Mexican immigrants make up the largest group of immigrants in the United States and are often the focus of debates about English language learners and bilingual education. It is this inability to speak English—or at the very least, their poor understanding of written and spoken English—that fuels the debate over what steps private businesses and the government should take so that English language learners can communicate with English and non-English speakers.

The controversy starts in the schools with the question of whether students should be taught in bilingual or English-immersion classrooms. Students enrolled in bilingual education receive instruction in the core subjects of math and science in their native language so they can keep up with their English-speaking peers. Their other classes are taught in English so that they can learn the language and gain proficiency in it. Proponents of bilingual education argue that children learn to read and write in their native language more easily than in English, and once they understand the concepts of reading, writing, and grammar, it is easier to transfer their knowledge over to English.

Opponents of bilingual education assert that immersion is the best way to learn, both school subjects and the English language. Immersion is just that—foreign-language students are completely immersed in English with all subjects taught solely in English. Supporters of immersion teaching maintain that children learn to speak, read, write, and think in English very quickly, and usually within six months they become comfortable enough with their new language that they will start using English outside of the classroom.

While children can usually learn another language easily when they are young, it is much more difficult for adults to learn a foreign language, especially a language as difficult as English. Generally, the older the adult, the more difficult it is to learn the language. Some immigrants never learn English: They may not have the time, money, or motivation to take English classes; English classes may not be available for them to take; or they may live in an isolated enclave filled with their countrymen and never need to speak English. As of 2008 no national law mandates that English is the official language of the country, although thirty states have passed legislation making English the official language in those states.

Some businesses have tried, with limited success, to require that their employees speak only English while at work. The Equal

Employment Opportunity Commission (EEOC), a federal agency that monitors businesses for illegal discriminatory practices, has strict rules on when English can and cannot be required at work. Generally, businesses can require employees to speak English for valid safety reasons, such as in fire and police departments, and among other emergency personnel, or if employees regularly come in contact with English-speaking customers. However, businesses cannot require employees to speak English just because their English-speaking employees do not like hearing a foreign language spoken.

Adult immigrants attend an English class in Florida. Generally, the older the adult, the more difficult it is to learn the language.

Assimilation is perhaps the most divisive issue concerning English language learners in the United States. Many Americans assert that immigrants cannot be assimilated into American culture unless they speak English. And yet many immigrants say they do not want to lose their culture, identity, or language by assimilating into the American melting pot. The articles in this anthology explore many of the issues involved with English language learners, bilingual education, and the English-only/official English movement, with the hope that the reader will come to understand the issues involved.

In addition, the volume includes a bibliography, a list of organizations to contact for further information, and other useful appendixes. The appendix titled "What You Should Know About English Language Learners" offers vital facts about those learning English as a second language and how this issue affects young people. The appendix "What You Should Do About English Language Learners" discusses various solutions to the problems of those learning to speak English. These many useful features make *Issues That Concern You: English Language Learners* a valuable resource. Given the growing costs of being a society in which multiple languages are spoken, having a greater understanding of this issue is critical.

ONE

Bilingual Teaching Is Beneficial to English Language Learners

Kelley Dawson Salas

> Kelley Dawson Salas is a fourth-grade teacher in Milwaukee, Wisconsin, and an editor for *Rethinking Schools*, a national magazine that examines the problems that schools face. In the following viewpoint she argues that students who are English language learners (ELLs) can benefit greatly from bilingual education. The author says that studies show that ELLs do better in school and on standardized tests when they learn in a bilingual classroom rather than in English-only programs. Salas maintains that students who are literate in their primary language have an easier time transferring their literary and academic skills to English. However, school districts, the states, and the federal government are pressuring schools and teachers to move students from bilingual classes to English-only classes before the students are ready, she says. Students then have less time to establish solid literacy skills in their primary language. If students do not have a good base in their primary language, they are unlikely to do well in English.

"Teacher, this is crazy!"

After six days straight of standardized testing in English, her second language, Ana lost it. She laughed out loud and the rest of us laughed with her. As her 4th-grade teacher I was expected to keep order and continue administering the test (which I did), but I could see where she was coming from. Perhaps it was the rigorous schedule: seven days of testing for three hours each morning. Perhaps it was the tedious format: listen as each test item is read aloud twice in English and twice in Spanish, then wait for all students to mark an answer, then move on to the next test item. Perhaps it was the random nature of some of the questions.

Whatever it was, Ana knew it didn't make sense. That moment has become a metaphor to me. There are more English language learners than ever in U.S. schools, and yet the policies that affect their schooling make less and less sense.

About 10 percent of all U.S. students—more than five million children—are English language learners. This represents a tremendous resource and opportunity. If schools serve English language learners well, at least 10 percent of U.S. students can have highly valued skills: fluency in more than one language and an ability to work with diverse groups of people. If communities give English-speaking students the opportunity to learn side by side with students who speak other languages, an even greater number of students can learn these skills.

But there are obstacles. Although research shows that bilingual education works, top-down policies increasingly push English-only education. To make matters worse, schools serving immigrants are some of the most segregated, understaffed, under-resourced schools in the country.

In our Winter 2002/03 editorial, *Rethinking Schools* wrote that "bilingual education is a human and civil right." I think all teachers should defend this right and demand equal educational opportunities for English language learners. It's not just about immigrant students: U.S. society as a whole will benefit greatly when all students have access to bilingual education, and when schools serve English language learners well.

Bilingual Education Works

Research shows that bilingual education is effective with English learners, both in helping them learn English and in supporting academic achievement in the content areas.

A synthesis of research . . . published by Cambridge University Press showed that English learners do better in school when they participate in programs that are designed to help them learn English. The review also found that "almost all evaluations of K-12 [kindergarten through grade twelve] students show that students who have been educated in bilingual classrooms, particularly in long-term programs that aim for a high level of bilingualism, do as well as or better on standardized tests than students in comparison groups of English-learners in English-only programs."

A synthesis of studies on language-minority students' academic achievement published in 1992 by Virginia Collier found that students do better academically in their second language when they have more instruction in their primary language, combined with balanced support in the second language.

I have seen this in action at the two-way immersion school where I teach 4th grade. Spanish-dominant students who develop good literacy skills in Spanish have a far easier time in 3rd and 4th grade when they begin to read, write, and do academic work in English. Likewise, students who struggle to read and write in Spanish do not transition easily to English reading, and they tend to lag behind in English content-area instruction. High-quality Spanish language instruction starting in kindergarten is essential. Without it, Spanish-dominant students do not get a fair chance to develop good literacy and academic skills in their first, *or* second language.

More Need, Less Bilingual Instruction

Despite the evidence that properly implemented bilingual education works for English language learners, English learners are being pushed into English-only programs or getting less instruction in their primary languages.

Voters in three states (California, 1998; Arizona, 2000; Massachusetts, 2002) have passed referenda mandating "English-only" education and outlawing bilingual instruction. (Colorado defeated a similar referendum in 2002.) Although many parents in these states hoped to get waivers so their children could continue bilingual education, they had more luck in some places than others.

In Arizona, one-third of English language learners were enrolled in bilingual education before voters passed Proposition 203 in 2000. Although Proposition 203 allowed waivers, the state's Superintendent of Public Instruction insisted on a strict interpretation of the law that denied waivers to most parents. Eventually almost all of Arizona's bilingual programs were discontinued; the National Association for Bilingual Education noted in October of 2005 that "bilingual education is simply no longer available" to English language learners in Arizona.

Prior to the passage of Question 2 in Massachusetts in 2002, 23 percent of that state's roughly 50,000 English learners were enrolled in bilingual education. By 2005, only about 5 percent were in bilingual programs. Under the new law it is easier for children older than 10 to get waivers, so middle and high school students are more likely to participate in bilingual education than elementary students. Students do not need a waiver to participate in two-way bilingual programs; in 2005 there were 822 students enrolled in two-way bilingual programs.

Resistance Saves Some Programs

In California, the first state to pass an English-only referendum in 1998, some schools were able to continue offering bilingual education. The law required all districts to inform parents of their option to continue in bilingual education by signing a waiver; some schools and districts succeeded in getting a very high percentage of waivers and continuing their programs. But by 1999, researchers at the University of California Linguistic Minority Research Institute found that only 12 percent of English learners were in bilingual programs, compared to 29 percent before the law changed.

Researchers also found that districts that had a strong commitment to primary language programs were able to hold on to those programs after Proposition 227 passed, while districts that were "not especially supportive of primary language programs prior to 1998" were more likely to do away with primary language instruction altogether.

The "English-HURRY!" Approach

Even in places where bilingual education is still permitted (by law or by waiver), top-down pressures threaten to weaken it. Since the passage of NCLB [No Child Left Behind Act], standardized testing in English has put pressure on schools to teach English earlier and to do it faster.

Because standardized tests are now administered in English, young ESL students are pushed to learn English before they have mastered literacy skills in their primary language.

Bilingual education is still legal in Wisconsin, where I teach. Milwaukee has a districtwide developmental bilingual (also called "late-exit") program. This means that children learn to read and write first in their primary language (in our case, Spanish), and in the early grades they are taught all subjects in Spanish. Once they have gained a strong footing in Spanish, they transition to English and start to receive a larger percentage of literacy and content area instruction in English. Even after making the transition to English, students can continue to get a significant portion of their literacy and content area instruction in Spanish for as many years as they choose to stay in the bilingual program.

But since the passage of NCLB, our district's developmental bilingual program has not fared as well as one might hope. In 2002, Wisconsin did away with all of its Spanish-language standardized tests and began requiring almost all English language learners to take standardized tests in English starting in 3rd grade. (Wisconsin could have purchased and administered tests in Spanish, but chose not to do so because of the cost.)

The English tests have changed classroom instruction for bilingual students in our district. District administrators, many principals, and lots of teachers have bought into the idea that kids must learn English sooner because they must score well on English language tests. "Hurry up and teach kids to read in English! They've got to be ready to take the 3rd-grade reading test in English! They've got to be ready to take the 4th-grade WKCE [Wisconsin Knowledge Concepts Exam] in English!" Suddenly a lot of what we know about second-language acquisition has fallen by the wayside in the scramble to get kids to do well on tests so we can keep schools off the list.

An Earlier Transition to English

At my school, the year after the law changed, I was part of a team of teachers and administrators that met for months to decide how to respond to the reality that our Spanish-dominant students would be tested in English starting in 3rd grade. We ultimately decided to transition children to English reading in the 2nd and 3rd grades. (We had previously transitioned students to reading in their second language at the end of 3rd grade and beginning of 4th grade.) Other schools in my district have also pushed the transition to English to earlier grades. Still others have reduced primary language instruction in the early grades to make room for direct instruction in English reading (for Spanish-speaking students) as early as 1st grade.

There has been little public discussion about these changes, which contradict the research because they decrease the amount of primary-language instruction and allow less time for students to establish solid literacy skills in their primary language before beginning the transition to second-language literacy. Instead of engaging in discussion about these changes, many administrators and some teachers dismiss concerns with a common refrain: "This is what we have to do to get them ready for the tests."

The Change in Bilingual Education

In a report called "The Initial Impact of Proposition 227 on the Instruction of English Learners," researchers in California described how bilingual instruction changed when English-only testing began:

> English-only testing was observed to have an extraordinary effect on English learner instruction, causing teachers to leapfrog much of the normal literacy instruction and go directly to English word recognition or phonics, bereft of meaning or context. Teachers also worried greatly that if they spent time orienting the children to broader literacy activities like storytelling, story sequencing activities, reading for meaning, or writing and vocabulary development in the primary language, that their students would not be gaining the skills that would be tested on the standardized test in English. They feared that this could result in the school and the students suffering sanctions imposed by the law.

> Thus, even in the classrooms that had been designated as bilingual, and where principals often contended that little had changed, teachers revealed that their teaching practices had indeed changed substantially and that their students

were receiving much less literacy instruction in their primary language.

Ironically, the NCLB does not specify what language students should be taught in, nor does it even require that students be tested in English. It specifies that students must be tested "in a valid and reliable manner," and that they should be given "reasonable accommodations," including "to the extent practicable, assessments in the language and form most likely to yield accurate data on what such students know and can do."

But states have chosen to implement the law in a variety of ways. Most states test students exclusively in English. Some states give English learners extra time to take the test. Another common accommodation is to translate or simplify the English on portions of the test. The state of California allows no accommodations for students who have been in the California schools

Most Common Accommodations for Bilingual Students

Accommodation	Number of States
Bilingual dictionary	32
Reading items aloud in English	32
Small group administration	29
Extra time	27
Individual administration	27
Separate location	25
Extra breaks	25
Directions in student's native language	24

Taken from: Government Accountability Office, "No Child Left Behind Act: Assistance from Education Could Help States Better Measure Progress of Students with Limited English Proficiency," July 2006.

for one year. Ten California districts have filed suit claiming this violates the NCLB's provision that students be tested in a valid and reliable manner with reasonable accommodations.

Segregation and Unequal Resources

These recent changes in language and testing policies are making a bad situation worse for English language learners, many of whom were already experiencing some of the worst educational conditions in the country.

A study published by the Urban Institute in September 2005 noted that the majority of English language learners [ELL] are "segregated in schools serving primarily ELL and immigrant children." The study found that these "high-LEP" schools (defined as schools where Limited English Proficient [LEP] students comprise 23.5 percent or more of the student body) tend to be large and urban, with a student body that is largely minority (77 percent) and largely poor (72 percent). In addition, "high-LEP schools face more difficulties filling teaching vacancies and are more likely to rely on unqualified and substitute teachers," and teachers are "more likely to have provisional, emergency, or temporary certification than are those in other schools."

Researchers at the University of California, Davis, in 2003 found similar disadvantages for the schooling of English language learners, saying they faced "intense segregation into schools and classrooms that place [English learners] at particularly high risk for educational failure."

Advocacy for Immigrants

As conditions and policies worsen for English learners, there is an urgent need for teachers, families, and language-minority communities to speak up in favor of immigrant students and bilingual education.

It is important for English learners to succeed academically and to become bilingual, especially now. Many U.S. cities have majority-minority populations, and more and more people in the United States speak languages other than English. To be able to successfully live in and lead this diverse society, people need to learn how to value and accept others. All children need to learn how to communicate with people whose language and culture are different from their own.

These abilities are highly valued, and many teenagers and adults spend years trying to develop them. Children who are raised from birth speaking a language other than English have a unique opportunity to cultivate these abilities from a young age. Our schools must help them seize that opportunity.

TWO

Bilingual Teaching Has Little Effect in Improving English Fluency

Greg Collins

Greg Collins was a student at the University of Massachusetts at the time this viewpoint was written. He writes that the goal of teaching bilingual students in their primary language to ensure that they keep up with their classmates who are taught in English is ineffective. Collins maintains that students who are taught in their primary language fall behind in the most important subject of all, English. Bilingual education may benefit students in the short term, but in the long term, he contends that bilingual students suffer because they have not been exposed to the difficulties involved with and the expectations of mastering English. Collins asserts that by learning English, immigrants enter into a covenant with other Americans to become completely assimilated Americans.

If any one policy trivializes and patronizes immigrants, it is bilingual education. Possible presidential hopeful Newt Gingrich re-ignited this issue . . . when he spoke to the National Federation of Republican Women in Washington [in 2007] . . . saying, "The American people believe English should be the official language of the government. . . . We should replace bilingual education with immersion in English so people learn the common language of the country and they learn the language of prosperity, not the language of living in a ghetto."

A Reexamination of Bilingual Education

As immigration reform has risen to be one of the leading and most contentious political topics confronting current politicians and presidential candidates, bilingual education deserves to be reexamined. Continuing to enforce this policy is counterproductive towards encouraging assimilation among immigrants, which hurts both themselves and the future of the United States.

The goal of bilingual education programs that teach students mathematics and reading in their native language, like Spanish, is to ensure they do not fall behind their classmates in these subjects. But attempting to keep pace with their classmates in this regard stunts their growth in learning the most important subject of all, which is of course English.

We are all aware of the benefits of becoming proficient in English, as it strengthens communication among all Americans and provides a deep bond to convey our feelings in a mutually comprehensible fashion. Taking into account tangible, real world benefits, mastering English enables immigrants to acquire the necessary skills to work at higher-skilled jobs to improve their socioeconomic status and to become financially independent. Immigrants will be able to start families and provide for them without depending on government programs.

But bilingual education supporters gloss over these facts by sacrificing long term ramifications for short term benefits. In the short run students will not face the difficulties and high expectations of mastering English. But when these people encounter situations in which proficiency in English is a necessary prerequisite to fulfill the task at hand, whether it is writing an essay in college or responding to a customer's request at a restaurant, they will be left behind by people who already know the language.

Some people contend that teaching subjects such as math and reading to immigrant students in their native language may limit their success as adults.

Long-Term Ramifications

Bilingual education supporters claim that they want to ease the transition of immigrants from their homeland to America. However, enforcing programs that de-emphasize the significance of a skill proven to be a crucial factor in earning high grades or getting hired does more to inhibit this transition than bilingual educators would care to admit.

We shouldn't lambaste employees or students who do not speak English very well when educators and politicians enact policies to reflect a concern for feeling good about other people rather than having a genuine concern for helping immigrants transition to America in the quickest possible fashion. It is entirely logical why immigrants would not absorb the English language as quickly as they would normally when politicians and School Board members discourage assimilation into American society. Why would individuals feel the need to learn English quickly when programs are designed specifically to inhibit this growth? Progressives claim their policies reflect the needs and wishes of immigrants and the poor, but it is programs like bilingual education that explicitly promote laziness and irresponsibility for failing to adapt to a new culture.

One must be reminded that enforcing mastery in English does not devalue or denigrate the language and customs of the

Comparing English-Language Proficiency and Language Arts Standards for Fifth Graders

English-Language Proficiency Standards	Language Arts Standards
The student can comprehend reading passages written in familiar or short sentence patterns and verbalize some of the main points of the passage.	The student can independently read and comprehend a grade-level-appropriate text and write a short essay describing the main idea of the text.
The student can use acquired knowledge of the English language to learn and understand new vocabulary in context.	The student can apply knowledge of reading strategies to comprehend the text of the next higher level of difficulty.

Taken from: U.S. Department of Education, "Final Non-regulatory Guidance on the Title III State Formula Grant Program—Standards Assessments and Accountability," February 2003.

immigrants' past. There are many language programs in the U.S. available for people who want to learn their native language.

But feeling neutral about whether or not to enforce proficiency in English undermines the roots which have provided the foundation for the rise and maintenance of America as the most unified nation in the world. Our Founding Fathers and the Puritans who formed the original communities of this country would have found it reprehensible if they were told that this nation's educators were subsidizing education primarily taught in Spanish or any language besides English.

A Covenant with Other Americans

Instead, mandating education taught exclusively in English affirms the uniqueness of a country that enables people of all different backgrounds to not only embrace the most commonly spoken language in this country. It also allows legal immigrants to enter into an implicit but deeply powerful covenant with other Americans who will help their newly assimilated Americans in times of need. This would be the seminal milestone for an immigrant who was attracted to America because of its freedoms and national unity.

Bilingual education is a tacit way of saying that only a certain group of people have the capabilities of becoming completely immersed Americans, and that immigrants should not be held up to the same standards as American-born children who also face the expectation of learning English.

The issue is not whether immigrants will struggle to learn English, because most assuredly they will. However, countless immigrants, including many of our descendents, have admirably confronted and conquered this challenge. Through the adaptation of learning English, immigrants have embraced American conceptions of morality, virtue, and liberal democracies. To expect anything less from immigrants is insulting and patronizing to their souls.

THREE

English Immersion Is the Best Way to Teach English Language Learners

Newt Gingrich

Newt Gingrich, Speaker of the U.S. House of Representatives from 1995 to 1999, is a senior fellow at the American Enterprise Institute and author of *Winning the Future: A 21st Century Contract with America.* In the following viewpoint, Gingrich argues that speaking a country's language opens doors of opportunity. In the United States claims Gengrich, English is the nation's language, and so all Americans should learn and speak English. The best way for new Americans to learn English, says Gingrich, is to replace bilingual education with intensive English instruction. Furthermore, all voting ballots and government documents should be in English, he says.

I've been taking lessons to learn Spanish for a while now, and it's given me a new understanding of how difficult it is to learn a new language. And there's no question that if I lived in a Spanish-speaking country and had to study and work and shop in Spanish as I struggled to learn the language, the challenges would be greater. But there's also no doubt that the rewards would be greater too. Mastering the language of a country opens doors of opportunity, plain and simple.

The Language of Success

In the United States, English is by no means our only language, but it is the language of economic success and upward mobility. More important, it is the language of our national unity and political discourse. And just as opportunity is the birthright of all native-born Americans, it becomes the inheritance of all new

Bilingual Students in the United States

About 94 percent of students who speak a language other than English at home live in fifteen states. Since 1998, three states—California, Arizona, and Massachusetts—have stopped offering bilingual education. Bilingual education is mandatory in Alaska.

State Where Bilingual Students Live	Number of Bilingual Students	Percentage of Bilingual Students
Alaska	30,000	1 percent
Arizona	200,000	7 percent
California	1,250,000	41 percent
Colorado	22,000	0.8 percent
Connecticut	20,000	0.6 percent
Florida	150,000	5 percent
Illinois	110,000	3.5 percent
Massachusetts	30,000	1 percent
Michigan	45,000	1.5 percent
Nevada	25,000	0.8 percent
New Jersey	50,000	1.5 percent
New Mexico	80,000	2.6 percent
New York	210,000	7 percent
Oklahoma	30,000	1 percent
Texas	450,000	15 percent

Taken from: "The Status of Bilingual Education in America," ProEnglish.org.

Americans. But this is nothing more than a nice sentiment if we don't do all we can to encourage and help new Americans learn English.

Among the ways we can do this as quickly as possible is to replace bilingual education programs in our public schools with intensive English instruction and abolish the federal mandates requiring multilingual ballots and government documents.

Passions sometimes run high when the topic is English. I learned that firsthand . . . because of a poor choice of words when talking about this subject. That's understandable. After all, there are 31 million Spanish speakers in the United States. There are also millions of Americans whose first language is Vietnamese, Korean, Chinese, Hindi or Farsi, to name just a few. They are all justifiably proud of their language and their cultural heritage.

Still, it's important that we not allow passion to rule the debate. Too often, sincere expressions of support for English as our unifying language are interpreted as a lack of support for welcoming and respecting new Americans. For example, those who support "English-first" are often mistakenly portrayed as supporters of "English-only." English-first supporters believe that English should be the official language of the government but that other languages are fine in communities and commerce. In contrast, English-only advocates want to outlaw all languages other than English.

Clearly, these two positions are very different. Promoting English-first is not—and should not be—disrespectful of other languages. In fact, supporting English instruction for immigrants demonstrates our confidence in their ability to pursue happiness here and contribute to their families, communities and new country.

A Call for Intensive Language Instruction

As a part of any comprehensive immigration reform, we should renew our commitment to making sure that all new immigrants have the opportunity to learn English. In public schools, children should have intensive English instruction rather than bilingual classes. For adults, we can adopt something similar to a program Israel has for its new immigrants. There, every new resident is

Newt Gingrich, former Speaker of the U.S. House of Representatives, argues that all Americans should speak English as their primary language.

entitled to 500 hours of intensive Hebrew language instruction paid for by the government. And along with intensive English language instruction, they could receive U.S. history and civics training.

Equally important, we must abolish federal rules requiring that government documents—including ballots—be printed in multiple languages. These multilingual documents discourage immigrants from learning English as rapidly as possible, limiting their ability to engage in a truly common political culture. Rather than expanding opportunities for new Americans, these mandates help limit them.

We must never lose sight of the self-evident truths affirmed at our founding: that we are all created equal—citizen and noncitizen alike—and that we are each endowed by our creator with certain unalienable rights, among them life, liberty and the pursuit of happiness. If we are to live out these truths, new immigrants deserve our respect, not our condescension. They deserve the opportunity to pursue happiness in the U.S. that comes with speaking English.

Meanwhile, I'm going to keep working on my Spanish. It's hard, but I'm making progress—poco a poco.

FOUR

All Students Should Receive a Bilingual Education

Teachers College, Columbia University

> Teachers College (TC), although affiliated with Columbia University, is a separate college that trains teachers and administrators. In the following viewpoint the college argues that language is a vital part of who people are, and so it is important to allow people to use their primary language when learning new skills and information. According to the author, research shows that allowing children to use their primary language is the most effective way to achieve higher levels of learning in school. Bilingual education has come under siege in American schools, TC argues, and bilingual proficiency has been discredited.

At Flushing International High School in Queens [New York], Humanities teacher Kevin Hesseltine recently kicked off a class on imperialism by scribbling the following direction on the blackboard: "Free Write: Has your native country experienced Imperialism? By who? Was it economic, political, social or all of the above? Give examples."

At a table of ninth and tenth graders, one boy, whose family had recently emigrated from China, appealed to his seatmates to clarify the question.

"Calling a Rose by Its Other Names," *Teachers College, Columbia University, Annual Report, 2007*, pp. 17–19. Reproduced by permission.

"Was your country ever invaded," explained a girl from Pakistan.

"Yes," the boy replied. "Japan."

He then called out, in Chinese, to several other Chinese boys, who suggested—in English—another possible invader: Mongolia.

And so it goes at Flushing International and its sister schools (eight in New York City and one in Oakland, California). Language is seen both as a tool of communication and as a way to draw on other strengths of the school's largely immigrant student population.

"Their language is a part of who they are as people, not just as learners," says Principal Joseph Luft. "You don't deny students a part of who they are or prevent them from using skills and abilities they have to learn. If someone sent you and me off to China but said, 'You can't speak to each other in English'—well, I think you can see the absurdity of it."

Rising Tide

The number of U.S. students classified as English language learners (ELLs) has at least doubled over the past 25 years, and now accounts for more than 10 percent of total public school enrollment. Collectively ELLs speak more than 460 languages, with the most common being Spanish, Vietnamese, Hmong Korean, Arabic, Haitian Creole and Cantonese. The U.S. has 10,000 young native speakers of Urdu alone. Overall, ELLs are enrolling in American public schools at a rate seven times the national average for all students.

Yet according to data from the National Assessment of Educational Progress (NAEP), only 4 percent of these "English language learners" in the eighth grade are proficient in reading and only 6 percent in math. Seventy-one percent of ELLs scored below "basic" on the eighth grade NAEP reading and math tests. ELLs trail English-proficient students by 39 points in reading and 36 points in math on a 500-point scale nationally. And a survey in 2003 revealed that 50 percent of ELLs fail their graduation tests, compared with 24 percent of English-proficient students.

Number of U.S. Immigrants Who Have Obtained Resident Status

1997–2001

Region of birth	1997	1998	1999	2000	2001
Total	797,847	653,206	644,787	841,002	1,058,902
Africa	47,732	40,585	36,578	44,534	53,731
Asia	265,674	219,371	198,918	264,413	348,256
Europe	119,764	90,572	92,314	130,996	174,411
North America	307,313	252,503	270,719	338,959	405,638
Oceania	4,340	3,922	3,658	5,105	6,071
South America	52,832	45,281	41,444	55,823	68,484
Unknown	192	972	1,156	1,172	2,311

2002–2006

Region of birth	2002	2003	2004	2005	2006
Total	1,059,356	703,542	957,883	1,122,373	1,266,264
Africa	60,101	48,642	66,422	85,102	117,430
Asia	340,494	243,918	334,540	400,135	422,333
Europe	173,524	100,434	133,181	176,569	164,285
North America	402,949	249,968	342,468	345,575	414,096
Oceania	5,515	4,351	5,985	6,546	7,385
South America	74,151	55,028	72,060	103,143	138,001
Unknown	2,622	1,201	3,227	5,303	2,734

Taken from: Office of Immigration Statistics, *Yearbook of Immigration Statistics: 2006*. Washington, DC: U.S. Department of Homeland Security (2007).

A Close-Minded Approach

To TC [Teachers College, Columbia University] faculty members Ofelia García and Jo Anne Kleifgen and doctoral student Lorriane Falchi, authors of the Equity Matters research review "From English Language Learners to Emergent Bilinguals," those failures stem from a fundamentally close-minded approach to language—and one that is very much at odds with mainstream thinking in other countries. In fact, while it may seem counterintuitive, research has shown that using a child's first language is the most effective way to help her achieve a higher level in an English language school system. "The benefits of such practices are explained by the concept of linguistic interdependence—the notion that two languages bolster each other and the student's ability to acquire knowledge," the TC authors write.

That's very much the thinking—and practice—at the Twenty-First Century Academy for Community Leadership, a predominantly Hispanic pre-k–8 [prekindergarten through grade eight] school located in Washington Heights. Beginning in kindergarten, where Margaret Blachley also uses sign language to help kids remember words, classes are taught in English one day, Spanish the next.

"We have signs to go with all of our routines, so the children become more comfortable with them," says Blachley who hit upon the sign language idea with a fellow teacher. "I don't have a scientific article to prove it, but I see them able to produce more language."

And where bilingual children at most U.S. schools typically abandon Spanish at the third or fourth grade, "that's where our kids flourish, because they have the power of Spanish to keep helping them," says Principal Evelyn Linares. She adds that her students not only go on to take New York State's Spanish regent exam, "but pass it and pass it with distinction."

To Ofelia García—a native Spaniard who, despite her multiple degrees and her flawless English, says she still sometimes feels intimidated walking into American schools—this is merely common-sense thinking.

"Throughout the world, bilingualism is the norm," says García, who heads TC's Center for Multiple Languages and Literacies.

"But here, bilingualism is the elephant in the room. In viewing non-native speakers simply as people who 'don't yet speak English' we're focusing only on the elephant's tail."

Paradigm Shift

It wasn't always that way. In the 1960s, the Bilingual Education Act established a federal goal of assisting limited English speaking students in the quick acquisition of English. In the early 1970s, in *Lau v. Nichols*, a group of Chinese-American parents brought a judicial case against the San Francisco school board that eventually went before the U.S. Supreme Court, successfully arguing that, by being thrown into English-only classrooms, ELLs were being (in the words of the Court's majority opinion) "effectively foreclosed from any meaningful education." The Court instructed school districts to take "affirmative steps" to address these inequities, but left the mode of instruction up to the educators.

Change Begins

Things began to change in the 1980s, when the focus of the Bilingual Education Act began to shift toward supporting programs that used only English in educating ELLs and that imposed time limits on participation in transitional bilingual education. In the 1990s, the use of children's native language to support learning came under political siege, perhaps best typified by Proposition 227, a California initiative that prohibits the use of native language instruction and mandates the use of sheltered English immersion programs, where students are mainstreamed into regular classrooms after just one year. And under the federal No Child Left Behind Act (NCLB), passed in 2002, the pressure to bring all students to reading and math proficiency by 2014 has led districts in many states to minimize the number of ELLs per grade in order to avoid having to report data on these students and sustain penalties if they haven't made sufficient average yearly progress.

García, Kleifgen and Falchi believe that these policy shifts have amounted to a "silencing of bilingualism and bilingual edu-

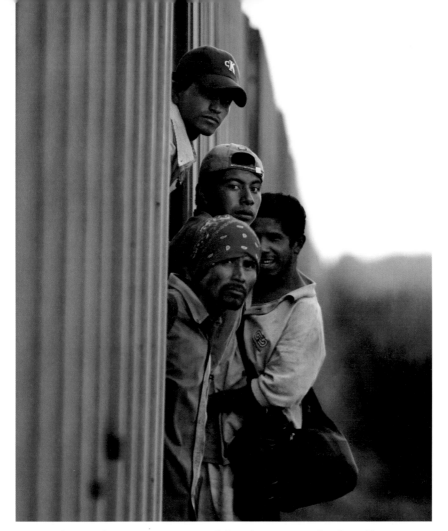

Spanish-speaking immigrants like these may find walking into an American school intimidating.

cation." They argue that the very term "English Language Learner" reflects all the failings in the U.S. approach and call instead for "emergent bilingual" as a preferable term for students in this population. "Calling them ELL is erasing who they are," García says. "They already contribute to our society with divergent thinking, a facility with languages—skills that we can use in the classroom and beyond."

At Flushing International High School, Kevin Hesseltine agrees. Earlier in the day, his students, asked to split into groups with different flags and divide up the classroom under their respective banners, spontaneously propose a diplomatic conference.

Later, Hesseltine, a Peace Corps graduate who speaks Ukrainian, says the benefits of the system are evident. "For me, this is the most interesting place to be teaching," he says. "American kids would never have gotten it. These guys can pull off what they know about their own countries. It's much more interesting to me. Every kid is so different."

FIVE

English Should Be the Official Language of the United States

Mauro E. Mujica

> Mauro E. Mujica, an immigrant from Chile, is chairman and chief executive officer of U. S. English Inc. U.S. English Inc. is the nation's oldest and largest citizens' action group dedicated to making English the official language of the United States. Mujica writes in the following viewpoint that English is the language of education, business, science, music, travel, the Internet, and diplomacy. Americans must be able to speak, read, and write English in order to succeed in life. He asserts that English should be made the official language of the United States, and all business—government, economic, or educational—should be completed in English. Bilingual or multilingual government or education comes at a high price that takes funds away from other important areas, such as health care, police and fire services, transportation, and education and could fuel ethnic or linguistic resentments, he argues. Declaring English as America's official language would force immigrants to learn it and would unify the country, according to Mujica.

In June 2003, the Pew Research Center announced the results of an extensive survey on global trends such as the spread of democracy, globalization, and technology. Titled "Views of a

Changing World," it was conducted from 2001 to 2003 and polled 66,000 people from 50 countries. The survey received some publicity in the United States, mainly because it showed that anti-American sentiments were on the upswing around the world. Less publicized was the fact that there is a now a global consensus on the need to learn English.

One question in the Pew survey asked respondents to agree or disagree with the statement "Children need to learn English to succeed in the world today." Many nations showed almost unanimous agreement on the importance of learning English. Examples include Vietnam, 98 percent; Indonesia, 96 percent; Germany and South Africa, 95 percent; India, 93 percent; China and the Philippines, 92 percent; Honduras, Japan, Nigeria, and Uganda, 91 percent; and France, Mexico, and Ukraine, 90 percent.

To an immigrant like myself (from Chile), these results come as no surprise. Parents around the world know that English is the global language and that their children need to learn it to succeed. English is the language of business, higher education, diplomacy, aviation, the Internet, science, popular music, entertainment, and international travel. All signs point to its continued acceptance across the planet.

Given the globalization of English, one might be tempted to ask why the United States would need to declare English its official language. Why codify something that is happening naturally and without government involvement?

The Retreat of English

In fact, even as it spreads across the globe, English is on the retreat in vast sections of the United States. Our government makes it easy for immigrants to function in their native languages through bilingual education, multilingual ballots and driver's license exams, and government-funded translators in schools and hospitals. Providing most essential services to immigrants in their native languages is expensive for American taxpayers and also keeps immigrants linguistically isolated.

Historically, the need to speak and understand English has served as an important incentive for immigrants to learn the language and assimilate into the mainstream of American society. For the last 30 years, this idea has been turned on its head. Expecting immigrants to learn English has been called "racist." Marta Jimenez, an attorney for the Mexican American Legal Defense and Educational Fund, speaks of "the historical use of English in the United States as a tool of oppression."

Groups such as the National Association for Bilingual Education complain about the "restrictive goal" of having immigrant children learn in English. The former mayor of Miami, Maurice Ferre, dismissed the idea of even a bilingual future for his city. "We're talking about Spanish as a main form of communication, as an official language," he averred. "Not on the way to English."

Perhaps this change is best illustrated in the evolving views of the League of United Latin American Citizens (LULAC). Started in 1929, the group was originally pro-English and pro-assimilation. One of the founding aims and purposes of LULAC was "to foster the acquisition and facile use of the Official Language of our country that we may hereby equip ourselves and our families for the fullest enjoyment of our rights and privileges and the efficient discharge of our duties and obligations to this, our country." By the 1980s the executive director of LULAC, Arnoldo Torres, could proudly proclaim, "We cannot assimilate and we won't!"

Limited English Proficient Americans

The result of this is that the United States has a rapidly growing population of people—often native born—who are not proficient in English. The 2000 Census found that 21.3 million Americans (8 percent of the population) are classified as "limited English proficient," a 52 percent increase from 1990 and more than double the 1980 total. More than 5 million of these people were born in the United States.

Citing census statistics gives an idea of how far English is slipping in America, but it does not show how this is played out in everyday life. Consider the following examples:

- The *New York Times* reports that Hispanics account for over 40 percent of the population of Hartford, Connecticut, and that the city is becoming "Latinized." Last year [2002], Eddie Perez became Hartford's first Hispanic mayor. The city Web page is bilingual, and after-hours callers to the mayor's office are greeted by a message in Spanish. Half of Hartford's Hispanics do not speak English. According to Freddy Ortiz, who owns a bakery in the city, "In the bank, they speak Spanish; at the hospital, they speak Spanish; my bakery suppliers are starting to speak Spanish. Even at the post office, they are Americans, but they speak Spanish." Even Mayor Perez notes that "we've become a Latin city, so to speak. It's a sign of things to come."

Limited English Proficiency in the Schools

- In May [2003], about 20 percent of the students at Miami Senior High School, where 88 percent of the students speak English as a second language, failed the annual Florida Comprehensive Assessment Test (FCAT) exam, which is required for graduation. The poor results prompted protests and demands for the test to be given in Spanish as well as English. Over 200 students and teachers gathered outside the school waving signs and chanting "No FCAT." A state senator from Miami introduced a bill that would allow the FCAT to be given in Spanish.
- Just a day before the Pew survey was released, Gwinnett County in Georgia announced it will provide its own staff translators for parents of students who speak Spanish, Korean, and Vietnamese. The school board approved $138,000 for the new translators despite a tight budget. Donna Robertson, a principal at an elementary school in the county, claimed the translators are only a short-term solution. The real solution, she claims, is a multilingual school staff. There are 46 languages spoken among students in Gwinnett County.
- In May [2003], a poll taken by NBC News and the *Sun-Sentinel* newspaper of Fort Lauderdale, Florida, found 83 percent of Hispanics in south Florida agreeing that "it is easy to get along day in and day out without speaking English well/at all."

The Cost of Multilingualism

Multilingual government is not cheap. Bilingual education alone is estimated to cost taxpayers billions of dollars per year. The fed-

Proponents of English-only laws cite the huge cost to taxpayers of providing bilingual services to immigrants in their native language.

eral government has spent over $100 million to study the effectiveness of bilingual education, only to discover that it is less effective at teaching English than English immersion programs are. Much of the cost for court and school translators, multilingual voting ballots, and multiple document translations is picked up at the local level. Even during good economic times, this is a burden. In lean years it is a budget breaker, taking funds away from education, health care, transportation, and police and fire services.

For example, Los Angeles County spent $3.3 million, 15 percent of the entire election budget, to print election ballots in seven languages and hire multilingual poll workers for the March 2002 primary. The county also spends $265 per day for each of 420 full-time court interpreters. San Francisco spends $350,000 per each language that documents must be translated into under its bilingual government ordinance. Financial officials in Washington, D.C., estimate that a proposed language access would cost $7.74 million to implement. The bill would require all city agencies to hire translators and translate official documents for any language spoken by over 500 non-English-speaking people in the city.

The health-care industry, already reeling from a shortage of nurses and the costs of treating the uninsured, was dealt another blow by President [Bill] Clinton. Executive Order 13166 was signed into law on August 11, 2000. The order requires private physicians, clinics, and hospitals that accept Medicare and Medicaid to provide, at their own expense, translators for any language spoken by any patient. The cost of an interpreter can exceed the reimbursement of a Medicare or Medicaid visit by 13 times—costing doctors as much as $500 per translator.

Of course, there are also nonmonetary costs associated with a multilingual America. These expenses often have a human cost.

The Cost to Human Lives

A 22-year-old immigrant won a $71 million settlement because a group of paramedics and doctors misdiagnosed a blood clot in his brain. The man's relatives used the Spanish word intoxicado to describe his ailment. They meant he was nauseated, but the translator interpreted the word to mean intoxicated.

Six children were killed when a loose tailgate from a tractor trailer fell off on a Milwaukee highway. The driver of the family's SUV could not avoid the tailgate, which punctured the gas tank and caused the vehicle to explode. An investigation found that other truckers had tried to warn the driver of the tractor trailer about his loose tailgate, but the driver did not understand English.

An immigrant in Orange County, California, died from a fall into a 175-degree vat of chemicals at an Anaheim metal-plating shop. Though the company's instructions clearly forbade walking on the five-inch rail between tanks, they were printed in English, a language that the worker did not understand. An inquiry into the accident found that many of the recent hires were not proficient in English.

Hispanics accounted for nearly one-third of Georgia's workplace deaths in 2000, despite making up only 5.3 percent of the state's population. The National Institute for Occupational Safety and Health, a branch of the U.S. Centers for Disease Control and Prevention, blamed "misunderstandings arising from language barriers" for the deaths and said they "could be prevented and don't have to happen."

The Dis-United States

We need only look to Canada to see the problems a multilingual society can bring. America's northern neighbor faces a severe

Canada's dual language requirements—English and French —have caused divisiveness and have also proved costly.

constitutional crisis over the issue of language. In 1995, the predominately French-speaking province of Quebec came within a few thousand votes of seceding from Canada. The secessionist Parti Quebecois ruled the province until this year. The national government must cater to Quebec to preserve order and maintain a cohesive government. This has spurred secessionist movements in English-speaking western Canada on the grounds that the Canadian government favors French speakers.

Of course, battles over language rage across the globe, but since Canada is so similar, it offers the most instructive warning for the United States. While the policy of official multilingualism has led to disunity, resentment, and near-secession, it is also very costly. Canada's dual-language requirement costs approxi-

States That Have Made English the Official Language

Hawaii (Hawaiian is also an official language.)

States in which the official language is English

Taken from: ProEnglish, "English in the 50 States," 2007.

mately $260 million each year. Canada has one-tenth the population of the United States and spent that amount accommodating only two languages. A similar language policy would cost the United States much more than $4 billion annually, as we have a greater population and many more languages to accommodate.

Unless the United States changes course, it is clearly on the road to a Canadian-style system of linguistic enclaves, wasteful government expenses, language battles that fuel ethnic resentments, and, in the long run, serious ethnic and linguistic separatist movements.

America's Unity at Stake

What is at stake here is the unity of our nation. Creating an American-style Quebec in the Southwest as well as "linguistic islands" in other parts of the United States will be a disaster far exceeding the Canadian problem. Now, over 8 percent of the population cannot speak English proficiently. What happens when that number turns to 10 percent, 20 percent, or more?

The American assimilation process, often called the melting pot, is clearly not working. Declaring English to be our official language would bring back the incentive to learn it. Specifically, this step would require that all laws, public proceedings, regulations, publications, orders, actions, programs, and policies are conducted in the English language. There would be some commonsense exceptions in the areas of public health and safety, national security, tourism, and commerce.

Of course, declaring English the official language would only apply to government. People can still speak whatever language they choose at home and in private life. Official English legislation should also be combined with provisions for more English classes for non-English speakers. This can be paid for with a fraction of the money saved by ending multilingual government.

A bill in Congress would make this a reality. The English Language Unity Act of 2003, H.R. 997, was introduced by Rep. Steve King (R-Iowa). . . . The bill already has over 90 cosponsors and is starting to make some waves on the talk radio circuit. If it passes, we can start to rebuild the American assimilation process and lessen the amount of linguistic separation in the United States. If it fails, we might have lost the last best chance for a sensible and cohesive language policy in this country. If that happens we can say hasta la vista to the "United" States and Adelante to Canadian-style discord over the issues of language and ethnicity. [Editor's note: The bill did not pass.]

SIX

Mandating English as the Official Language of the United States Is Unnecessary

James Crawford

> James Crawford is the director of the Institute for Language and Education Policy, an organization that uses research to advocate for English language learners. The following viewpoint is Crawford's testimony before Congress about making English the official language of the United States. Crawford argues that making English the official language is unnecessary, punitive, and divisive. Furthermore, official language legislation is also pointless, inconsistent with American values, and self-defeating. He believes that instead of English-only laws, the United States should embrace "English Plus," in which Americans become proficient in English as well as other languages.

My name is James Crawford. I am director of the Institute for Language and Education Policy, a newly formed nonprofit organization dedicated to research-based advocacy for English-language and heritage-language learners. We represent professionals in the field of language education who are working to promote academic excellence and equity for these students.

James Crawford, "Official English Legislation: Bad for Civil Rights, Bad for America's Interests, and Even Bad for English," Testimony Before the House Subcommittee on Education Reform, July 26, 2006. Reproduced by permission of the author.

I want to thank [you] for the opportunity to present testimony regarding proposals to designate English as the official language.

We at the Institute believe that such legislation is ill-advised: harmful to individuals, to the nation, and to the goal of language learning. We are concerned that the U.S. Senate recently passed a "national language" amendment without holding a single hearing to consider its potential impact and with only limited debate. So we commend the Subcommittee on Education Reform for convening [this] hearing in the House.

Reasons to Oppose Official English Legislation

In our view, "official English" is:

(1) *Unnecessary*—The overwhelming dominance of English in the United States is not threatened in any way. Newcomers to this country are learning it more rapidly than ever before. Our language does not need "legal protection."

(2) *Punitive*—Restricting government's ability to communicate in other languages would threaten the rights and welfare of millions of people, including many U.S. citizens, who are not fully proficient in English.

(3) *Pointless*—Official-English legislation offers no practical assistance to anyone trying to learn English. In fact, it is likely to frustrate that goal by outlawing programs designed to bring immigrants into the mainstream of our society.

(4) *Divisive*—The campaign to declare English the official language often serves as a proxy for hostility toward minority groups, Latinos and Asians in particular. It is exacerbating ethnic tensions in a growing number of communities.

(5) *Inconsistent with American values*—Official-English laws have been declared unconstitutional in state and federal courts, because they violate guarantees of freedom of speech and equal protection of the laws.

(6) *Self-defeating*—English Only policies are foolish in an era of globalization, when multilingual skills are essential to economic prosperity and national security. Language resources should be conserved and developed, not suppressed.

Critics of mandating English as the official language of the United States say it is divisive and promotes hostility toward minority groups.

Language and Liberty

Our nation has gotten by for more than 200 years without adopting an official language. So the obvious question arises: Why do we need one now?

Proponents of official English have responded with platitudes ("A common language is what unites us as Americans") or truisms ("In this country it's essential to know English") or anxieties ("Spanish is spreading at unhealthy rates") or unsupported claims ("Bilingual programs discourage people from learning English"). These are not compelling arguments. They also reflect an ignorance of history.

Language has been far less central to American identity than to, say, French or Greek or Russian identity. From its infancy the United States was conceived as a nation that newcomers could join, whatever their ethnic background, simply by swearing loyalty to the democratic principles on which it was founded. To be sure, there have been ugly episodes of language-based discrimination, such as the English Only school policies that once targeted Native Americans and Mexican Americans. Unlike many other countries, however, we have seldom passed laws to repress or restrict minority tongues. Language has usually been taken for granted here—as a practical rather than a symbolic issue—despite the diversity that has historically prevailed.

Today there are more non-English languages spoken in America than ever before, owing to the ease of travel, which has brought immigrants from all over the world. But the *proportion of minority language speakers* was certainly as large, if not larger, in 1776, 1865, and 1910. Where immigrant groups were numerous and enjoyed political clout, they were often accommodated in their own vernaculars. Until the early 20th century,

Language Spoken at Home and English-Speaking Ability, 2000

All speakers, age 5+	262,375,152	100 percent
English only	215,423,557	82 percent
Other language	46,951,595	17.9 percent
Speaks English "very well"	25,631,188	9.8 percent
Speaks English "well"	10,333,556	3.9 percent
Speaks English "not well"	7,620,719	2.9 percent
Speaks English "not at all"	3,366,132	1.3 percent

Taken from: James Crawford "Official English Legislation: Bad for Civil Rights, Bad for America's Interests, and Even Bad for English," Testimony Before the House Subcommittee on Education Reform, July 26, 2006. [2000 Census of Population]

state and local governments provided documents and services in languages such as German, French, Spanish, Swedish, Norwegian, Welsh, and Czech. Bilingual education was more widespread in German and English in 1900 than it is today in all languages.

Despite or—more likely—because of these tolerant policies, immigrant groups gradually adopted English and stopped speaking their ancestral tongues. Sociologist Nathan Glazer has noted the irony: "Languages shriveled in the air of freedom while they had apparently flourished under adversity in Europe." Except in a few periods of nativist hysteria, such as the World War I era, laissez-faire policies made language conflicts relatively rare in the United States.

No Threat to English

Is there any reason to abandon our tradition of tolerance now? Certainly there is *no threat to English* in America, no challenge to its status as the language of educational advancement, economic success, and political discourse. According to the 2000 census, 92% of U.S. residents speak English fluently; 96% speak it "well" or "very well"; and only 1.3% speak no English at all.

Demographic research also shows that, while the number of minority language speakers is increasing, largely because of immigration, the rate of Anglicization is also on the rise. Immigrants at the turn of the 21st century are learning English—and losing other languages—more rapidly than those at the turn of the 20th.

Official English is truly a "solution in search of a problem."

All Stick and No Carrot

While official-English proposals vary, those now pending before Congress take a radical, restrictionist approach. They would not merely celebrate "our common language." In addition, they would prohibit most uses of other languages by the federal government —whether to communicate information, provide services, or enable limited-English speakers to exercise rights they would otherwise enjoy.

The assumption is that English Only policies would create an incentive to learn English by making life as difficult as possible for those who have yet to do so. Yet where is the evidence that the current patchwork of basic services in other languages provides a *dis*incentive to English acquisition? How many immigrants say to themselves, for example, "If I can read pamphlets about Social Security in Spanish or visit a bilingual health clinic or rely on a court interpreter if I'm charged with a crime, why should I worry about learning English?" Don't limited-English speakers face language barriers in countless other situations on a daily basis? It would be irresponsible for Congress to legislate without empirical data in this area, considering that millions of people could be adversely affected.

English-as-a-second-language instruction, by contrast, has proven quite effective in helping adult immigrants learn the language. Yet, to date, no official-English bill has included any provisions to address the chronic shortage of such classes in most parts of the country. *Coercion, not empowerment,* is the operative principle here. . . .

Without exception, the bilingual assistance programs now provided by government are designed to safeguard the rights and serve the needs of limited-English speakers so as to help them acculturate. Those who are thereby brought into the mainstream are more able and more inclined to learn English than those remaining on the margins of society, unable to access government services. While English Only advocates seem intent on making a symbolic statement, their proposals would have very practical consequences in areas such as education, social services, civil rights, and government efficiency. Among other things, their proposals are bad for English acquisition.

A Message of Intolerance

The symbolic statement itself has consequences that are as damaging as the direct legal effects. English Only bills say, in effect, that the principles of free speech and equal protection apply only to those who are fully proficient in English; that discrimination on the basis of language is legitimate, even laudatory in America;

and ultimately, that those from non-English backgrounds are unwelcome here.

Whatever "message" the sponsors believe they are sending with this legislation, the message received is a message of intolerance. This phenomenon is evident in the *language vigilantism* that occurs every time the issue flares up, as local officials and individuals seek to impose their own English Only rules. Here are a few of the mean-spirited incidents that occurred after the House passed a "language of government bill" in 1996:

- Tavern owners in Yakima, Washington, refused to serve patrons who conversed in Spanish, posting signs such as: "In the U.S.A., It's English or Adios Amigo."
- A judge hearing a child-custody case in Amarillo, Texas, accused a mother of child abuse for speaking Spanish to her five-year-old daughter.
- Police in Yonkers, New York, ticketed a Cuban American truck driver for his inability to answer questions in English.
- In Huntsville, Alabama, the county assessor refused to approve routine tax exemptions for Korean property owners whose English was limited.
- Norcross, Georgia, authorities fined the pastor of a Spanish-speaking congregation for posting placards that allegedly violated an English Only sign ordinance.

Fueling Race Hatred

These acts are deeply offensive, not only to recent immigrants, but also to a broader population: persons who are proud of their heritage both as Americans and as ethnic minorities. As Senator Mel Martinez, a Cuban immigrant and a Republican from Florida, . . . explained: "When they start saying that it's un-American to have ballots printed in Spanish, it sends a message that we're not wanted, not respected."

No doubt this is the message that some extremists *intend* to send—or to exploit—in hopes of building support for a restrictive immigration policy. In doing so, they are dividing communities across the nation. [In July 2006] the city council of Hazleton, Pennsylvania, coupled an official-English ordinance with harsh penalties for businesses that hire or landlords who rent to undocumented immigrants. The result has been to exacerbate tensions between longtime residents and recently arrived Latinos who are clearly being targeted. Similar proposals are fueling race hatred in municipalities from Avon Park, Florida, to San Bernardino, California.

It's ironic that official-English legislation, promoted as a way to "unite Americans," is having precisely the opposite effect: igniting ethnic conflicts. Congress should refuse to fan these flames.

Monolingualism Is an Economic Handicap

The aftermath of September 11 [2001] highlighted a longstanding concern of national security officials: the United States remains an underdeveloped country where language skills are concerned. When our military invaded Afghanistan to hunt down al Qaeda, five of that country's seven major languages—including Pashto, spoken by 8 million Afghans—were not even taught in U.S. colleges and universities. Meanwhile, the FBI [Federal Bureau of Investigation] was so desperate for translators of Arabic and the languages of south Asia that it was forced to place want-ads in newspapers, with problematic results.

Monolingualism, for which Americans are justifiably notorious, is also an economic handicap. While English is indisputably dominant in global commerce, it is spoken by only a small minority of the world's population. As globalization increases, competitors who are proficient in other languages will have an increasing advantage.

The President's National Security Language Initiative, designed [by George W. Bush] to fund programs in critical languages such as Arabic, Chinese, Hindi, Russian, and Farsi, is a positive step. His proposed investment, however—$114 million in FY07 [fiscal year 2007], including just $24 million at the K-12 [kindergarten through grade twelve] level—is ludicrous. If approved, it would have a limited impact relative to the nation's growing needs.

Instead of English Only . . . English Plus

Yet this is not just a funding problem. More important, it is an *attitude problem*. While a language learned in the classroom is valued in this country, a language learned by growing up in a minority community is likely to be considered a liability, not an asset. "Ethnic bilingualism" has enormous potential to supply the multilingual skills that America needs. Rather than cultivating it, however, we rush language-minority children into all-English classrooms as soon as possible. Most never get the chance to develop advanced skills, including literacy, in their native tongue. Although *developmental bilingual education* does exist, it is getting much harder to find. High-stakes testing in English for these students and, in some states, English Only instruction laws have forced schools to dismantle many bilingual programs.

Instead of English Only, the United States needs a language policy that could be described as *English Plus*. This approach begins with the recognition that, of course, we should pursue the goal of English proficiency for all Americans. But while English is necessary, it is not sufficient in today's world. To prosper economically and to provide security for our people, we need well developed skills in English, plus other languages. Step one is to conserve and develop, not destroy, the language resources we already have. Rather than treating bilingualism as a nuisance or a threat, we should exploit our diversity to enrich the lives of individuals and foster the nation's interests, while encouraging ethnic tolerance and safeguarding civil rights.

We believe that a policy of English Plus would advance these important goals. Official English would be a step backward for the nation.

SEVEN

Demand for English Classes Outstrips Supply

Gaiutra Bahadur

Gaiutra Bahadur, a reporter for *The Philadelphia Inquirer*, wrote the following article in which he examines the demand for and supply of English language classes for immigrants. He cites statistics that show there are not enough resources to fill the demand for English language classes and students are turned away. While enclaves in nearly every city exist where people do not have to speak English to get by, most people want to learn English, says Bahadur. People realize that life is much harder in the United States if they do not speak English.

The hullabaloo over the signs at Geno's Steaks has been fed by a perception that many immigrants don't want to, try to or have to speak English.

That perception is so fierce and deep that elected officials at every level have reacted: The U.S. Senate voted [in May 2006], to make English the national language as part of its proposed immigration overhaul. The coal-country town of Hazleton, Pa., just passed an English-only ordinance. And President George W. Bush, in an address in May [2006] urged newcomers to learn English to "honor the great American tradition of the melting pot."

He was proselytizing the converted, judging by the demand among adult immigrants for English classes—a demand that has been outpacing funds for such instruction.

"You close your mind. You close all the opportunities for your life" without English, said Ruben Del Rosario.

The 27-year-old Mexican immigrant lives near the now world-famous Geno's signs that exhort, "This is America. When ordering, please speak English."

That is just what Del Rosario has been trying to do since coming to the United States six years ago. He picked up the word cocky from sportscasters riffing on Sixers games. He puzzled over the word nappy, overheard on the streets of Philadelphia. And he attends English classes three hours a day, five mornings a week.

About 1.2 million adults take English for Speakers of Other Languages (ESOL) classes subsidized partly by the state and federal government and typically run by civic groups, community colleges, churches and even unions. Others take classes funded by charitable groups; still more pay for-profits to school them.

Not Enough English Language Classes

The classes are full to the brim, pushed there by growing numbers of immigrants who are isolated by language. Ten years ago, Philadelphia's Center for Literacy had a few English classes for adult immigrants. Now it has 16 classes and 400 students.

One in four people speaking a foreign language at home wants to study English but can't because of a lack of time, child care, money or transportation, according to the National Center for Education Statistics.

At the same time demand has risen, state and federal funds for adult-education programs, which include English for immigrants, have stagnated. The budget for one program, Even Start, was halved last year and faces more cuts in 2007.

"There aren't enough resources to teach all the people who want to take English classes," said Liza Rodriguez, an ESOL teacher for a decade.

Juntos, a Mexican community association in South Philadelphia where Del Rosario studies English, gets no government money for

Recent immigrants attend an English as a second language course in Brooklyn, New York. Some people argue that there are not enough resources available to teach all those who want to learn English.

its small, volunteer-taught classes. It applied for funding through the state but was told there was no more, organizer Peter Bloom said.

More groups are applying for federal and state adult-education grants distributed by the Pennsylvania Department of Education, said spokesman Brian McDonald.

"We've had to turn them away," he said. "We can't necessarily take on more of a load."

Despite the growing need, the department has awarded the same yearly amount for ESOL classes since 2002: about $8 million, or one-third of all its money for family literacy.

Funding for English classes at ACLAMO (Accion Comunal Latinoamericana de Montgomery County), a community service agency, has dropped from $119,000 to $98,000 over the last five years.

"We're stuck having to raise more private dollars," said Justin Fink, its associate director of education programs. The agency used to serve 20 families through Even Start. Now it serves 18.

A health crisis with her baby daughter drove Norma Flores, 21, to ACLAMO's classes a year ago.

"We went to the emergency room, and sometimes nobody spoke Spanish," the mother of four explained in English. "The doctor needs to know if she drink the medicine, if she has a fever, and I couldn't tell him."

"I feel . . . ," Flores said, straining to find the words. Her teacher, Maria Benssy, pulled out a binder and indicated a page with emoticons. Flores found the ones that applied: "I feel 'stressed out.' I feel 'sad.'"

Most of ACLAMO's English students are women from impoverished rural areas in the Mexican state of Puebla. About a third balance classes with work and child-rearing. Many were forced to drop out of elementary school, some as early as the third grade.

"It's one thing to teach English when it truly is a second language," said Benssy, an ESOL teacher for 15 years. "It's another thing when they have no idea not only what a tense is, but what a verb is. . . . They really are up against huge odds, and it's amazing that they get it."

Mandates to Use English

To skeptics, it might be striking that immigrants even want to get it. Twenty-seven states have passed ballot initiatives or bills making English the official language for government business. A similar legislative effort is underway in Harrisburg.

Those who want to mandate the use of English, whether from state capitals or from cheesesteak row, say that society does not force immigrants to speak English the way it did a century ago.

Federal Protections

Limited-English speakers now have federal protections. The Civil Rights Act of 1964 bars discrimination based on national origin. Under Title VI of that act, recipients of federal money must take "reasonable steps" to give "meaningful access" to services for those with little English, according to 2002 Justice Department guidelines.

But enforcing those guidelines is a battle, said Paul Uyehara, a lawyer at Community Legal Services in Philadelphia.

"You could walk down the street, and there are violations left and right," he said.

The Philadelphia Police Department, for one, was in danger of losing federal funds until last fall, when it started training officers to use qualified interpreters to talk to victims and suspects.

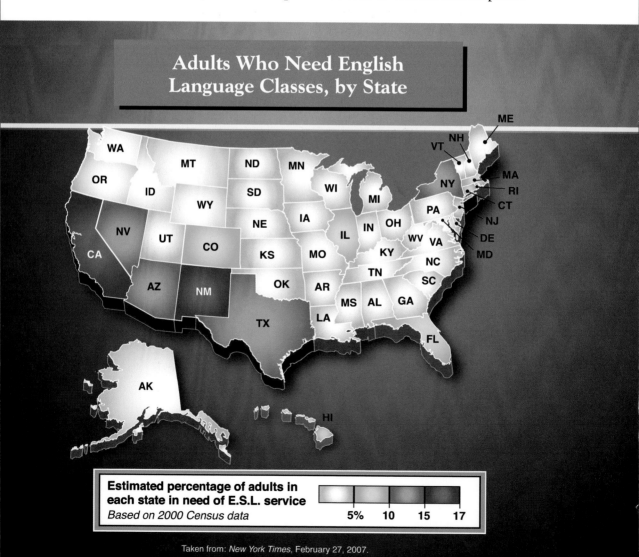

Adults Who Need English Language Classes, by State

Estimated percentage of adults in each state in need of E.S.L. service

Based on 2000 Census data

5%   10   15   17

Comfort Zones for Non-English Speakers

Also, neighborhood comfort zones remain for non-English speakers, on small scales such as South Philadelphia's nascent Little Mexico and on large ones such as Miami-Dade County in south Florida.

"In almost any language in the U.S., you can find an enclave," said Benssy. "You can get through your life speaking only Korean in some parts of Lansdale [Pennsylvania] or Philadelphia."

A Korean woman here for three decades finally went to Benssy's class in Glenside so she could communicate with her grandson.

"Some people come here at an old age, and it's very difficult to master the language, but most people want to speak English," said Marina Lipkovskaya, a teacher at the New World Association.

Her nonprofit teaches English to 700 adults in Bensalem and Northeast Philadelphia, areas crowded with Russian-speaking doctors, auto mechanics and insurance agents.

West Marshall Street in Norristown, home to ACLAMO, is an enclave in the making. The street is studded with signs in Spanish. They advertise Las Mejores Botas de Mexico ("the best boots from Mexico"), apartments for rent, children's clothes, DVDs and phone cards.

Adelita's Mexican Market carries *Maxim* en espaol, a telenovela magazine, a book about migrant deaths on the border and erotic comics—all in Spanish. A Spanish-English dictionary stands out in the mix.

Nearby, an African American barber has posted a written sign in Spanish. It translates to: "Victor the barber. There's a Mexican here to serve you."

Even in this linguistic cocoon, Andres Rosas, a cook at a Buca di Beppo restaurant who has been in this country six years, realized he needed to learn English. He enrolled in ACLAMO's program with his son 1 1/2 years ago.

"When you don't speak English," he said, "always it's very hard."

EIGHT

The Number of English Classes Is Adequate

U.S. English Foundation

The U.S. English Foundation is a nonprofit organization that supports English as the official language of the United States. It also provides information on teaching English to immigrants, sponsors educational programs, and represents official English advocates in court. It is a separate organization from U.S. English Inc. In the following viewpoint, an issue briefing published by the U.S. English Foundation, the organization contends that the "shortage" of English classes for immigrants is a myth. The organization claims that it is likely that immigrants sign up for English classes sponsored by several organizations and when they get into one class, they never remove their names from the other classes. Organizations are unlikely to actively remove names from their waiting lists, as the list is a sign of a healthy business and can be used to support requests for additional funding. Finally, the organization claims that the waiting periods of two weeks to up to a year are relatively short and are hardly cause for concern.

When discussing the state of assimilation in the United States today, many point to the staggering numbers of immigrants on waiting lists for English classes as evidence that cur-

U.S. English Foundation, "The Waiting List Myth," *U.S. English Foundation, Inc.*, 2007, pp. 2–7.

rent generations are on the road to becoming Americans. The length of these waiting lists, often given in the thousands, has been the subject of newspaper articles and talk shows, and some have seized upon it to declare that we need to put a nationwide focus on English classes above all.

> There is no shortage of motivation to learn. Instead, the extreme demands for ESL [English as a second language] services far exceed the available supply of open classes. Eager students join thousands of others greeted by lengthy waiting times that range from 12 to 18 months for the largest ESL providers in Albuquerque and Phoenix, up to three years or more in Boston and other northeastern cities. [Congressional Hispanic Caucus, *Letter to the Subcommittee on Education Reform of the Committee on Education and the Workforce, July 26, 2006.*]

> In my own State of Colorado, as I look at some of the statistics on the number of people who are waiting in long lines to learn English, it is an incredibly long line. In the five-county Denver-Metro area, adult ESL programs working with the Department of Education have 5,000 people enrolled in those programs. They have a waiting list that is up to 2 months, because there are so many people in the Denver metropolitan area who want to learn English. *Sen. Ken Salazar, debate on Amendment 4064 to S. 2611, 18 May 2006*

No person familiar with the issue can deny that English classes are necessary in the United States. In a nation where more than 10 million people speak English not well or not at all, some level of funding for language classes must be available. Demand is exceeding supply in many U.S. cities, and the issue of language acquisition must be addressed.

However, the use of the waiting list as a concrete example of the shortage of English classes is not the trump card that many people make of it. In fact, upon examination of the issue, the existence of waiting lists for English classes can hardly be seen as problematic. In *The Waiting List Myth*, we take a look at some of these facts in the hope that a fleshing out of this subject will allow us to concentrate on the more important issues at hand.

Scenario

Imagine that a couple wants to go out to dinner one evening. They call their favorite local restaurant, only to find that reservations are not available until 9 P.M. They are disappointed by the late time, but make the reservation because it will hold their place.

Even with that reservation made, its inconveniences drive the couple to consider other options. They call another restaurant, and when they find out that an 8 P.M. reservation is available, they seize this opportunity too. Still, they do not cancel the first reservation, leaving their options open and keeping alive the chance to go to their first choice in dining.

At 6 P.M., after a long day of working around the house, the couple decide that they are too tired to go out to dinner and too hungry to wait until 8 P.M. They pick up something locally and call it a night.

Plenty of Americans might call and cancel the reservation, but many more will not, as evidenced by the standard airline practice of "overbooking" flights. If this is how Americans fluent in English behave, it is likely that those who are limited English proficient will be even less likely to cross their name off of a waiting list. This creates two waiting list issues, "perpetual waiters," and "multiple waiters."

Perpetually in Waiting

When immigrants determined to learn English approach prospective programs, it is likely they follow the same path as the couple seeking a restaurant reservation. The student will visit one location, put his name on the waiting list, try the next location, add his name again in the hope of getting into the program with the quicker opening, and so on. In the end, the student will be on several waiting lists, or he might find an available class and still be on several waiting lists. Even as time goes on, those waiting lists remain. The person may have gotten into another class, left the area or lost interest, but their name will still appear on the waiting list.

Given the funding and staff levels of most English teaching programs, it is highly unlikely that program directors will expend time or effort to determine final outcomes of the persons on the wait list. Furthermore, the short nature of the classes make it highly likely that the only follow-up will be a reminder about the next registration period, not news of a class opening.

One Person, Multiple Lists

The example above also demonstrates how, in the case of a widely available commodity, one couple can appear on multiple lists,

Though there are waiting lists to attend ESL classes, some contend that the number of English classes being taught is adequate.

even if they eventually choose another option altogether. Absent a cost and requiring only the most basic of personal information, the couple in the story have filled four spots on a "waiting list" at two local restaurants. Yet in the end, they use none of them.

Examples of this are not limited to restaurants. Each year, millions of high school seniors apply to multiple colleges, even though it is impossible to attend more than one at the same time. State University will receive thousands of applications, accept some, wait list some and reject some. University of State also will receive thousands of applications, accept some, wait list some and reject some. These lists are by no means mutually exclusive.

For English classes, which can take place at the local university, the community center, the church, and many other locations, it is incomprehensible to think that a determined English learner is going to try one place, then be satisfied with being on the waiting list solely at that location. If the desire to learn English is strong, the immigrant will continue to seek available opportunities, much like Americans continue to seek the dinner reservation that meets their needs.

In the end, the immigrant may be happily enrolled at the English class at the Springfield Cultural Center. Yet at the same time, his name still appears on the "waiting list" at four churches, three private programs and one community center.

The Benefits of a Waiting List

Though customers may despise being on a waiting list, the existence of such a list is the sign of healthy business. There can be little doubt about the financial health of a restaurant where customers are always clamoring for a table. Similarly, the existence of a wait list at a university indicates that it has its pick of the best students.

The popularity of a program resulting in a wait list means that customers can be urged to make purchases and enrollment decisions immediately. Whether it is football tickets or concert tickets, prospective buyers can be pressured to "Buy NOW!" or "Be there early for the best seats!" In the end, the business benefits from quicker income generation and fewer hours required to generate that income.

For those programs which seek government and private funding, such as education classes, the existence of a wait list is concrete proof that they need additional assistance. A smoking cessation program that always has enough space to accommodate interested students is going to have a much harder time requesting more funding from government and private sources than a smoking cessation program with a waiting list of 50 persons. While the former must explain new programs or new developments in order to justify the extra expense, the class with the waiting list need only to point to a roll of names. It benefits these type of programs to have as long a list as possible, and in an arena with many additions and few subtractions, long lists are easy to grow.

The Growth in Waiting Lists

And grow they do. Here are several published examples of waiting list numbers from across the United States:

- In Boston, 3,500 adults were on waiting lists for English classes in 2004, according to the Massachusetts Department of Education. The same agency says that 17,000 people are on waiting lists statewide.
- In Arizona, the Arizona Department of Education found that 5,009 adults were on a waiting list to get into English classes and that an additional 5,686 were turned away in 2004.
- In 2003, the three largest programs in the Houston area had a combined waiting list of 12,000, according to Federico Salas, assistant state director of Texas Learns, the state office of adult education.
- In May 2006, there were 2,200 people on waiting lists for English-language programs in Montgomery County, Md., according to the County's Council.

Something Is Askew

These numbers are high, and fittingly, they are meant to propel us to act. Yet if we step back and consider the numbers, we may have more questions before proceeding.

- In June 2006 testimony before Congress, Dr. James Thomas Tucker of the National Association of Latino Elected and Appointed Officials Education Fund told a committee that there were 16,725 adults on ESL waiting lists in Boston. Yet less than two years earlier, the *Boston Globe* announced that there were 3,500 adults on waiting lists in Boston, and 17,000 in the entire state.
- In 2004, the Massachusetts Department of Education said that 17,000 people are on waiting lists statewide. Nine years earlier, the same agency said that there were 15,000 people on waiting list for English classes statewide. The increase of only 2,000 on the ESL waiting list is surprising, since the state's foreign born and limited English proficient population increased by more than 75,000 people over this period.
- In 1995, 68 volunteer literacy organizations reported a statewide waiting list of 1,846 people for English classes in Illinois. That same year, the waiting list in Colorado was 2,000–3,000, and was 6,000 in Dallas. According to the U.S. Census, there were roughly 800,000 limited English proficient persons living in Illinois, 200,000 in Colorado and 300,000 in Dallas at this time.

In defense of the varying numbers, the wide range of programs offering English lessons, their small staff size, and informal record keeping play a major role in the failure to come up with concrete numbers. Yet if the data record is woefully incomplete, it is inexcusable to mention these eye-popping numbers without issuing strong reservations about their validity.

Everybody Waits

There is little doubt that demand for English classes outstrips supply, and there is ample proof that wait lists exist across the United States. However, while we may sympathize with those who cannot get what they want right away, waiting is by no means a crime. It is part of life.

When Americans call up their doctor for a physical, they often wait weeks for an appointment. High school seniors who are wait listed for college know what is it like to be in a holding pat-

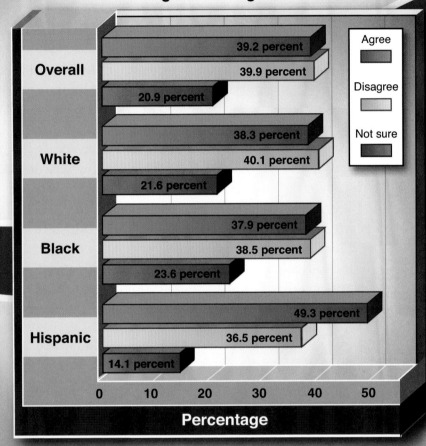

Are There Enough English Classes?

The U.S. government does not do enough to help immigrants learn English.

Agree or Disagree?

Overall
- 39.2 percent
- 39.9 percent
- 20.9 percent

White
- 38.3 percent
- 40.1 percent
- 21.6 percent

Black
- 37.9 percent
- 38.5 percent
- 23.6 percent

Hispanic
- 49.3 percent
- 36.5 percent
- 14.1 percent

Agree

Disagree

Not sure

0 10 20 30 40 50

Percentage

Taken from: Zogby International poll, March 2006.

tern. Then there is the most famous waiting list of all—the one for sports tickets.

According to various published sources, the New York Jets have a season ticket waiting list of 10,000 names. The Denver Broncos have a list of names exceeding 24,000. For the New England Patriots and Washington Redskins, the waiting list is 50,000 names. The longest list, that of the Green Bay Packers, have a season ticket waiting list that exceeded 70,000 names as of August 2006. On this long list, the estimated time between entering a name on the list and receiving tickets is 40 years.

Compared to these cases, the waiting list for ESL classes is far shorter. According to the testimony to Congress provided by Dr. James Thomas Tucker of the National Association of Latino Elected and Appointed Officials Education Fund, here are some of the wait times that prospective ESL students face:

- Two weeks to two months to enter ESL classes provided by seven schools in the Denver Area, according to the Colorado Department of Education
- Two weeks to six months in Seattle
- An average of one to three months in Newark, N.J.
- One to twelve months in Philadelphia, where only half the providers recorded any waiting list at all
- One to twelve months in New Haven, Conn.
- An average of two months in Las Vegas
- Up to six months in Chicago

If this is the evidence of problems with long waiting lists, it is hardly a cause for concern. With tax refunds on a turnaround time of at least two weeks, passport renewals requiring a wait time of six weeks and naturalization processes that can take years, a 60-day wait for an English class is not evidence of a severe problem.

Especially When It Is Free

Outside of the oft-discussed English classes, many of the items that involve waiting come with a cost. A college or university puts a student on a waitlist despite the knowledge that the institution stands to gain tuition income (and likely, future alumni gifts) if the student is accepted. Passport renewal requires six weeks even though the Department of State requires payment at the time of application. Considering that there are thousands of football fans just waiting to pay thousands of dollars for season tickets, it should hardly come as a surprise that there are thousands of people waiting for free or low-cost English classes.

Such is the case with any reduced price offering. When a certain ice cream company offers "free cone day," that company's stores are likely to experience longer customer wait times than its competitors. Certain online retailers offer free shipping on purchases over a specified dollar limit, but this option is only available with the slowest method of shipping. Goods that are needed sooner must be paid for at the faster shipping rate. It follows that English classes which have lower costs are going to have longer waiting lists.

Cost is hardly the only issue, however. Flexibility—both in location and time—also plays a major role. Convenience determines cost in many ways, as evidenced by the price differences between gas stations conveniently located on the highway and those a few miles off the main strip, or the price of bread at the corner convenience store and the supermarket on the edge of town. However, this flexibility also plays into the determination of waiting time.

Prospective English students who have transportation are more likely to be able to find an open English class than those that are limited to those available via public transportation routes. Additionally, those who can take classes during the morning and afternoon hours are also more likely to find openings than those who are limited to the evening hours. . . .

Final Words

It is clear that the current use of the "waiting list" as a concrete example of a problem that needs fixing is much like pointing to a patch of yellow grass and declaring a drought. Waiting lists, a natural by-product of a popular, yet low-cost program, cannot be seen as a definitive indication of the number of people looking to attend English classes. The ease of entry onto the list, combined with the ease of opportunity to find other options have left us with numbers that fail to correlate with the populations they claim are underserved. Moreover, it is clear that many of these wait periods fall within reasonably expected norms. These wait times may be inconvenient, but cannot be described as out of the ordinary.

Just as waiting lists at restaurants are not indicative of mass hunger and waiting lists at colleges fail to correlate to hordes of woebegone teenagers, waiting lists for English classes do not mean huddled masses of immigrants outside the local community center. As such, the limited English proficient population should not be pictured as hopelessly standing in line.

Few would disagree that English classes remain an important channel through which immigrants can make strides toward becoming Americans, even as Americans remain divided as to the funding sources for these classes. However, this debate on funding and need has become muddled up in a discussion of "waiting lists," a discussion which poorly correlates with the actual demand.

NINE

English-Only Laws Do Not Help Immigrants Gain Fluency in English

John Trasviña

John Trasviña is the president of the Mexican American Legal Defense and Educational Fund (MALDEF). MALDEF is the leading Latino advocacy and education organization that works to safeguard the civil rights of Latinos in the United States. The following viewpoint is Trasviña's testimony to Congress about a proposed English-only law. Trasviña asserts that English-only laws do nothing to promote English proficiency among immigrants and are bad policy. He claims that Latino immigrants are learning English faster than previous generations of immigrants, and that by the third generation, most Latinos speak only English. What is needed to achieve more and better English proficiency among immigrants are more English classes, not English-only laws.

No one, particularly a newcomer to America, needs a law or constitutional amendment to know that learning English is vital to participating in, contributing to, and succeeding in American society.

John Trasviña, "Statement of John Trasviña, Interim President and General Counsel, Maldef," Committee on Education and the Workforce U.S. House of Representatives 109th Congress, July 26, 2006. Reproduced by permission of the author.

English-only laws do nothing constructive to advance the important goal of English proficiency. Historically, we as a nation and as a people were correct to reject English-only, without at all minimizing the importance of education in English. English-only laws jeopardize the health, safety and well being not only of English language learners [ELL], but of American communities as a whole.

Bad Public Policy

Laws that interfere with the government's ability to communicate are simply bad public policy. Such laws fuel divisiveness and leave all of us more vulnerable to danger, and yield no discernible benefit. They do not promote English as our official language so much as they make discrimination our official language.

English-only is founded upon the myth that the English language is somehow under a threat. . . . An overwhelming majority, 92 percent of Latinos, believe that teaching English to the chil-

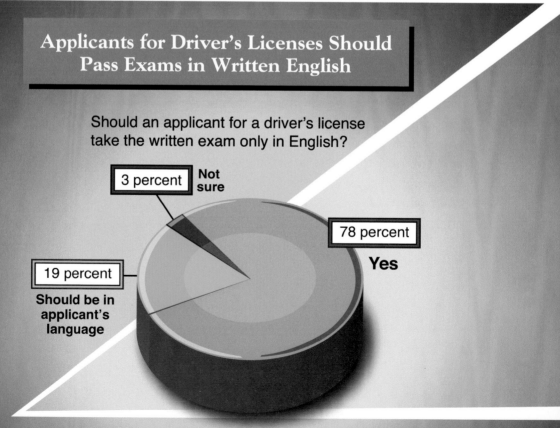

Applicants for Driver's Licenses Should Pass Exams in Written English

Should an applicant for a driver's license take the written exam only in English?

3 percent — Not sure

78 percent — Yes

19 percent — Should be in applicant's language

Taken from: Zogby International, March 14–16, 2006.

dren of immigrants is very important, a percentage far higher than other respondents.

Indeed, Latino immigrants are learning English and doing so as quickly or more quickly than previous generations of immigrants. As is typical of immigrant populations in the U.S., by the third generation most Latinos tend to speak only English. Latino immigrants, then, do not need official English or English-only legislation to coerce them into learning English. That desire and determination already runs deep in the Latino community.

They do, however, require the means and the opportunity. I would note . . . legislators do not need an English-only law to give them the impetus to provide classes for adult English. That is something that no legislator needs and it is not being done. That is one of the failings of these English-only laws.

Limited Opportunities

For ELL students in grades K [kindergarten] through 12, two-thirds of whom are native-born U.S. citizens, poor instruction denies them the tools to gain the language skills necessary to participate fully in the American economy and society. Since 1975, at least 24 successful education discrimination cases have been brought on behalf of ELL students in 15 states.

With limited opportunities to learn English, these students face particularly poor outcomes. It is critical that we improve programs for these students to help them learn English, not penalize them for the poor quality of instruction that denies them the opportunity to learn the language well.

Adults who seek English as a second language classes also face an acute shortage of such classes. A June, 2006 study by the NA-LEO [National Association of Latino Elected and Appointed Officials] Educational Fund found tremendous unmet need and waiting periods of up to 3 years. Providing real opportunities to learn English is the most efficient and effective means of fostering English language proficiency.

English-Only Laws Do Not Foster Fluency

By contrast, official English laws . . . do nothing to help them achieve fluency. Instead, such proposals compromise the health, safety and well being not only of English language learners, but of communities in which they live. These laws undermine the Federal Government's ability to communicate with the public in situations where communication is urgently needed, leaving all U.S. residents more vulnerable to danger.

I have heard about all the exceptions of the English-only laws. What you are left with after all these exceptions is that there is very little that the law actually covers. What it does not cover is more resources and opportunities for learning English.

Silly and Divisive Laws

When Dade County, Florida enacted an anti-bilingual ordinance in the 1980's, something that U.S. English supported at the time, its implementation underscored the silliness, divisiveness and danger of English-only laws. The first thing that went were the species signs at the zoo, because they were not in English. Then the county clerk stopped allowing translations of marriage ceremonies. Perhaps the most significant to health and safety, Jackson Memorial Hospital ended prenatal classes in Spanish and patient billing information.

At the federal level, there is no exemption on its Form 1040 for people who do not speak English. They, too, are taxpayers. Indeed, the IRS [Internal Revenue Service] has some of the best language services because they promote compliance and revenue. During wartime, the Treasury Department regularly promoted the selling of war bonds in many languages. Patriotism, after all, comes in all languages.

The push for English-only policies today and the hostile climate in which they have arisen are hardly unique in America's history. Fueled by anti-German sentiment during and after World War I, many states, including Iowa, passed English-only laws that sought to restrict the use of foreign languages in public. Hamburgers became Salisbury steaks. I understand the city of Berlin, Iowa became Lincoln, Iowa and the Iowa Governor ordered telephone operators to interfere with conversations in German.

But it took the U.S. Supreme Court in 1923 to address the English-only laws in Nebraska and in Iowa to state that the pro-

Juan Figueroa, president of the Puerto Rican Legal Defense and Education Fund, speaks at an anti–English only rally in Connecticut.

tection of the Constitution extends to all, to those who speak other languages as well as to those born with English on the tongue, and perhaps it would be highly advantageous if all had ready understanding of our ordinary speech.

But that cannot be coerced with methods which conflict with the Constitution. A desirable end cannot be promoted by prohibited means. We must do more to provide the availability and quality of English acquisition programs.

TEN

English-Only Policies in the Workplace Discriminate Against Workers

Charlton McIlwain and Stephen Maynard Caliendo

Charlton McIlwain is an assistant professor of culture and communication at New York University. Stephen Maynard Caliendo is associate professor of political science at North Central College in Illinois. They are both associated with the Race Project, a Web site that collects and disseminates research and information about race and politics in the United States. The following viewpoint is from their blog, in which they examine a discrimination lawsuit filed by the Equal Employment Opportunity Commission against the Salvation Army. The Salvation Army fired two workers for continuing to speak Spanish to each other after they had been told to learn English, even though they had no contact with customers and had been speaking Spanish at work for years. According to the authors, rules requiring English-only at work are a form of discrimination based on the worker's national origin. The prohibition against speaking Spanish has nothing to do with legitimate business reasons and everything to do with the employer's prejudice and negative feelings toward the employee's country of origin, the authors argue.

Charlton McIlwain and Stephen Maynard Caliendo, "Permissible Discrimination: The View from Congress," Raceproject.org, November 26, 2007. Reproduced by permission of the authors.

I t's okay to discriminate. So long as those you're discriminating against are generally poor (that is, can't afford to lose a job), native Spanish speakers, Mexican, and have the extreme gumption to speak anything but the king's English when they are at work.

This is essentially what the U.S. Congress said [in November 2007], as it continues to hold hostage the annual appropriation for the U.S. Equal Employment Opportunity Commission (EEOC) until it capitulates on the issue of litigating cases of employment discrimination based on national origin.

Congressional Audacity

How is it, you might ask, that Congress can reasonably demand that the agency charged with being the legal watchdogs of

On May 15, 2002, President George W. Bush signed the Notification and Federal Employee Antidiscrimination and Retaliation Act. The legislation prohibits discrimination and retaliation against employees of federal agencies.

workplace discrimination simply not do its job? Congress did, after all, write and pass the Civil Rights Act of 1964, Title VII of which prohibits employers from discriminating against employees on the basis of, among other things, one's national origin.

The EEOC has long held the position that language issues are closely related to issues of national origin, whether the case in point is a matter of accent, language fluency, or an English-Only requirement. It is a position echoed by the Court in 1989 when a 9th circuit ruling declared that accent and national origin are "obviously inextricably, intertwined," and require a "very searching look" in regard to employment decisions—in this case, on the linguistic basis of accent in particular. We'll return to the policy issue and distinctions surrounding English-Only litigation in a moment.

For the time being, however, let's focus on the general and specific answers to this question about Congressional audacity in dictating what forms of workplace discrimination the EEOC can and cannot litigate. The general answer is that our current discourse surrounding immigration has become a myopic debate not about immigration per se, in either principle or practice, but about illegal immigration. This would not be as much a problem were it not for the fact that our discussion about illegal immigration is largely a racialized discourse, fueled by opinion leaders in the media whose "news reporting" has been channeling our entire surplus of racial intolerance, bigotry and fear among the American public into a misguided attack on Mexican immigrants living and working in the U.S.

"Illegal" and "Immigration"

In the year preceding the attacks, there were roughly 500 or so newspaper stories where the issue of illegal immigration as it relates to Mexico appears. That number fell to just under 300 in the year following the terrorist attacks of 9/11 [2001]. In 2003 the number is 283, 329 the year following, and 539 the year after that. This number exploded to a whopping 1,535 in 2006.

At this height in 2006, a random search of newspaper reporting shows that the actual terms "illegal" and "immigration" are used in close proximity almost 50% of the time that the issue of immigration is discussed (surely the tenor of many of the others where the actual terms are not used is also focused on the issue of illegal immigration). Again, in 1996 (in a separate search), when the terms "illegal" and "immigration" are used together in the same paragraph in a news story, in 44 instances the story referred primarily to the Middle East. In 92 instances the subject was primarily Europe, about the same as the 94 instances where Canada was the focus of the discussion about illegal immigration. How many of the stories during the same time period focused on Mexico? 1,744.

This is far from scientific evidence, but it suggests that the fear, paranoia, prejudice and hatred of people who are not "us" following the September 11 attacks was used to resurrect an old enemy, while at the same time beginning the fight against a new one. When it came to foreign policy, we took the opportunity to take the fight to the Muslim world; when it came to domestic policy, we took the opportunity to focus on a different "threat"— Mexicans—who ostensibly come to this country for the sole purpose of stealing our jobs, taking advantage of our liberal welfare benefits, perpetrating violent crimes, and, last but not least, corrupting our national identity by corrupting our language.

A Political Pundit's Tirade

This is the general answer to why Congress seems hell bent on curbing English-Only litigation. The more specific answer is simpler. It comes down to a particular case of alleged national origin discrimination perpetrated by the Salvation Army, and a political pundit dressed in a newsman's clothing—Lou Dobbs. When the EEOC announced back in April of this year [2007] that it filed suit against the charitable organization, no one was more incensed than CNN's Lou Dobbs, who has become a veritable one-trick pony when it comes to news coverage/opinion-spewing on the issue of illegal immigration.

Upon hearing the news, Dobbs immediately responded in characteristic fashion. He "reported" the news with more than an air of sarcasm, misrepresented the facts of the case, blew the case out of proportion, challenged EEOC officials to a debate, and then claimed a moral victory when those officials did what is presumably common procedure—refuse to debate the details of a case that is currently in litigation.

First, Dobbs insinuated that the EEOC views any and every form of English-Only rule as discriminatory on the basis of national origin, therefore making it illegal under Title VII. The EEOC however has been quite clear that such policies are appropriate and legal, under certain circumstances, namely when there is a legitimate business reason for the policy—for example, in certain circumstances when an employee in a service industry is required as a function of their job to interact with English-speaking clientele.

The Salvation Army Case

The case against the Salvation Army, however, involved native Spanish speakers who worked as clothes sorters. They labored just fine with the Salvation Army for years, until the organization decided to enforce an old English-Only policy. In effect, the allegation by the EEOC is that national origin—expressed in the prohibition against speaking Spanish—has nothing to do with legitimate business reasons and everything to do with the negative sentiments of the employer about the employee's country of origin.

Second, from Dobbs's reporting of the story, one would think that this is the only form of discrimination the EEOC spends its time litigating. However, of the cases where the agency found a "reasonable cause" of discrimination, only 13% were cases of national origin discrimination, and it's likely that of these, even fewer were claims of language or English-Only policy discrimination.

What Dobbs was equally incensed about was the fact that the alleged discrimination was being done by the Salvation Army—a "Christian" charity. For Dobbs, nothing better personifies the bigotry and fear he spews on a daily basis about godless and immoral illegal immigrants who threaten the moral sanctity and Christian values inherent in our national identity than the government going after a Christian charity for insisting its employees speak English.

Discourse Gone Awry

It was this nationalistic and moralistic fervor that took hold of Republican members of Congress (beginning with Lamar Alex-

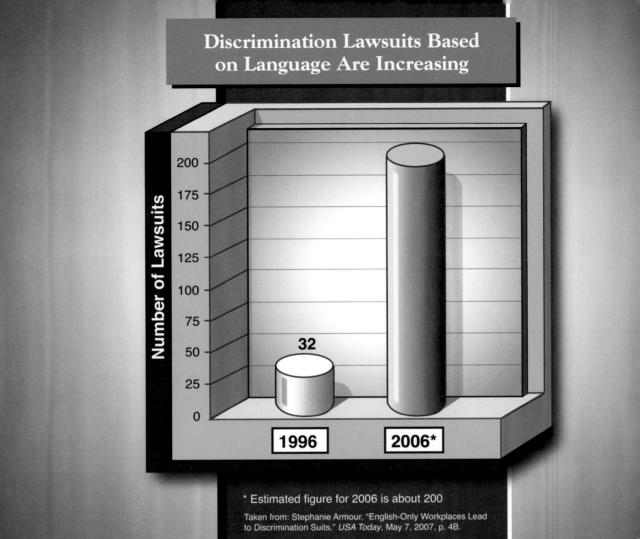

Discrimination Lawsuits Based on Language Are Increasing

Number of Lawsuits

200
175
150
125
100
75
50
25
0

32

1996

2006*

* Estimated figure for 2006 is about 200

Taken from: Stephanie Armour, "English-Only Workplaces Lead to Discrimination Suits," *USA Today*, May 7, 2007, p. 4B.

ander) eager to reassert the party's position as the standard-bearer of traditional American (Christian) values, as well as some Democratic members of Congress fearful not so much of Mexican immigrants as they are of losing the next election.

This continuing fight in the Congress about prohibiting the pursuit of discrimination claims based on national origin is but one of the prominent expressions of how the contemporary discourse about immigration policy has gone awry. Framing the general discourse about immigration policy around a racialized threat to American national identity will certainly hamstring our representatives from upholding one of the supposed principles of this identity—equal opportunity and equal protection under the law.

ELEVEN

English-Only Policies in the Workplace Help Workers Assimilate

John Fund

John Fund, an author and political journalist, wrote this column for *The Wall Street Journal*, in which he discusses the lawsuit filed by the Equal Employment Opportunity Commission against the Salvation Army, which fired two workers for speaking Spanish on the job. Fund asserts that rules requiring workers to speak English are perfectly reasonable; speaking multiple languages can easily lead to miscommunication and misunderstandings among the workers. Furthermore, if workers are allowed to speak different languages, the workplace—and society—can become polarized. Immigrants have a responsibility to assimilate into American culture, and speaking English is a great way to do that, says Fund.

Should the Salvation Army be able to require its employees to speak English? You wouldn't think that's controversial. But House Speaker Nancy Pelosi is holding up a $53 billion appropriations bill funding the FBI, NASA and Justice Department solely to block an attached amendment, passed by both the Senate and House, that protects the charity and other employers from federal lawsuits over their English-only policies.

The U.S. used to welcome immigrants while at the same time encouraging assimilation. Since 1906, for example, new citizens have had to show "the ability to read, write and speak ordinary English." A century later, this preference for assimilation is still overwhelmingly popular. A new Rasmussen poll finds that 87% of voters think it "very important" that people speak English in the U.S., with four out of five Hispanics agreeing. And 77% support the right of employers to have English-only policies, while only 14% are opposed.

But hardball politics practiced by ethnic grievance lobbies is driving assimilation into the dustbin of history. The House Hispanic Caucus withheld its votes from a key bill granting relief on the Alternative Minimum Tax until Ms. Pelosi promised to kill the Salvation Army relief amendment.

Obstructionism also exists on the state level. In California, which in 1998 overwhelmingly passed a measure designed to end

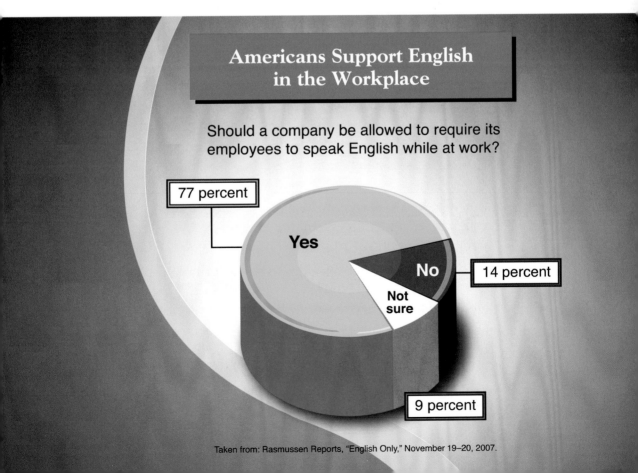

Americans Support English in the Workplace

Should a company be allowed to require its employees to speak English while at work?

77 percent — Yes

No — 14 percent

Not sure

9 percent

Taken from: Rasmussen Reports, "English Only," November 19–20, 2007.

bilingual education, the practice still flourishes. Only 29% of Latino students score proficient or better in statewide tests of English skills, so seven school districts have sued the state to stop English-only testing. "We're not testing what they know," is how Chula Vista school chief Lowell Billings justifies his proposed switch to tests in Spanish.

Yet the public is ready for leadership that will forthrightly defend reasonable assimilation. California Gov. Arnold Schwarzenegger won plaudits when he said last June that one way to close the Latino learning divide was "to turn off the Spanish TV set. It's that simple. You've got to learn English." Ruben Navarette, a columnist with the *San Diego Union-Tribune*, agreed, warning that "industries such as native language education or Spanish-language television [create] linguistic cocoons that offer the comfort of a warm bath when what English-learners really need is a cold shower."

Suing the Salvation Army

But the Equal Employment Opportunity Commission, the federal agency that last year filed over 200 lawsuits against employers over English-only rules, has a different vision. Its lawsuit against the Salvation Army accuses the organization of discriminating against two employees at its Framingham, Mass., thrift store "on the basis of their national origin." Its crime was to give the employees a year's notice that they should speak English on the job (outside of breaks) and then firing them after they did not. The EEOC sued only four years after a federal judge in Boston, in a separate suit, upheld the Salvation Army's English-only policy as an effort to "promote workplace harmony." Like a house burglar, the EEOC is trying every door in the legal neighborhood until it finds one that's open.

In theory, employers can escape the EEOC's clutches if they can prove their policies are based on grounds of safety or "compelling business necessity." But most companies choose to settle rather than be saddled with the legal bills. Synchro Start Products, a Chicago firm, paid $55,000 to settle an EEOC suit against its English-only policy, which it says it adopted after the use of

In 2006 the Equal Employment Opportunity Commission brought suit against the Salvation Army for discriminating against two employees at their Framingham, Massachusetts, thrift store.

multiple languages led to miscommunication. When one group of employees speak in a language other workers can't understand, the company said, it's easy for personal misunderstandings to undermine morale. Many companies complain they are in a Catch-22—potentially liable to lawsuits if employees insult each other but facing EEOC action if they pass English-only rules to better supervise those employee comments.

Diversity at the Expense of Unity

Sen. Lamar Alexander (R., Tenn.), who authored the now-stalled amendment to prohibit the funding of EEOC lawsuits against English-only rules, is astonished at the opposition he's generated. Rep. Joe Baca (D., Calif.), chair of the Hispanic Caucus, boasted that "there ain't going to be a bill" including the Alexander language because Speaker Pelosi had promised him the conference committee handling the Justice Department's budget would never meet. So Sen. Alexander proposed a compromise, only requiring that Congress be given 30 days notice before the filing of any EEOC lawsuit. "I was turned down flat," he told me. "We are now celebrating diversity at the expense of unity. One way to create that unity is to value, not devalue, our common language, English."

That's what pro-assimilation forces are moving to do. TV Azteca, Mexico's second-largest network, is launching a 60-hour series of English classes on all its U.S. affiliates. It recognizes that teaching English empowers Latinos. "If you live in this country, you have to speak as everybody else," Jose Martin Samano, Azteca's U.S. anchor, told Fox News. "Immigrants here in the U.S. can make up to 50% or 60% more if they speak both English and Spanish.

This is something we have to do for our own people."

Azteca isn't alone. Next month, a new group called Our Pledge will be launched. Counting Jeb Bush and former Clinton Housing Secretary Henry Cisneros among its board members, the organization believes absorbing immigrants is "the Sputnik challenge of our era." It will put forward two mutual pledges. It will ask immigrants to learn English, become self-sufficient and pledge allegiance to the U.S. It will ask Americans to provide immigrants help navigating the American system, the chance to eventually become a citizen and an atmosphere of respect.

This is a big challenge, but Our Pledge points out that the U.S. did it before with the Americanization movement of a century ago. It was government led, but the key players were businesses like the Ford Motor Company and nonprofits such as the YMCA, plus an array of churches and neighborhood groups.

Polarization

The alternative to Americanization is polarization. Already a tenth of the population speaks English poorly or not at all. Almost a quarter of all K-12 students nationwide are children of immigrants living between two worlds. It's time for people of good will to reject both the nativist and anti-assimilation extremists and act. If the federal government spends billions on the Voice of America for overseas audiences and on National Public Radio for upscale U.S. listeners, why not fund a "Radio New America" whose primary focus is to teach English and U.S. customs to new arrivals?

In 1999, President Bill Clinton said "new immigrants have a responsibility to enter the mainstream of American life." Eight years later, Clinton strategists Stan Greenberg and James Carville are warning their fellow Democrats that the frustration with immigrants and their lack of assimilation is creating a climate akin to the anti-welfare attitudes of the 1990s. They point out that 40% of independent voters now cite border security issues as the primary reason for their discontent.

In 1996, Mr. Clinton and a GOP Congress joined together to defuse the welfare issue by ending the federal welfare entitlement. Bold bipartisan action is needed again. With frustration this deep, it's in the interests of both parties not to let matters get out of hand.

TWELVE

English-Only Ballots Are Discriminatory

Asian American Legal Defense and Education Fund

The Asian American Legal Defense and Education Fund (AALDEF) is a national organization that promotes and protects the civil rights of Asian Americans, focusing on voting rights, among others. The following viewpoint is a report published by AALDEF in which it discusses Section 203 of the Voting Rights Act, which requires language assistance for voters with limited English proficiency (LEP). Many LEP voters may have voted with English ballots in the past, but they feel more comfortable voting in their own language, AALDEF argues. The voting process can be complicated; permitting voters to vote in their own language allows them to make informed choices, the Fund says.

Shiny Liu, a Chinese American voter from Queens County, New York, is limited English proficient. Although she has voted with English ballots in the past, she explained that she is more confident when she votes in her own language because she can be sure she understands her vote. Ms. Liu is 1 of 5 Asian American voters, represented by AALDEF [Asian American Legal Defense and Education Fund], who sued the New York City Board of Elections in February 2006 for pervasive violations of the language assistance provisions of Section 203. She described her voting experiences to illustrate why translated ballots and voting materials are still necessary:

> The first time I voted was in 2003. I used an interpreter and a ballot that was translated into Chinese. Now, I know how to vote, so I vote alone without any assistance. I have voted on ballots in English before, but I am not comfortable doing so because I am not confident that I properly understand the English. I would rather vote on ballots translated into Chinese because I can be sure of who and what I am voting for.

AALDEF's multilingual exit polls reveal that Ms. Liu's preference for translated ballots and voting materials is a common sentiment among Asian American voters. As Ms. Liu expressed, a ballot can be overly complicated to understand when the voter is limited English proficient. Indeed, even a native-born, English-speaking voter can be confused by the highly sophisticated content of lengthy referenda, or the technical instructions for casting a provisional ballot. Confusing ballots and instructions, in fact, contributed to the Florida recount in the 2000 [presidential] elections.

Difficulties in Learning English

Moreover, contrary to opponents of language assistance, language minority voters understand the importance of learning English and use the provisions as a means of participating in the democratic process. However, because of their financial circumstances, family obligations, or lack of access to English classes, not every Asian voter has the opportunity to learn the English language.

Henry Yee is an LEP [limited English proficient] voter who arrived in the United States 42 years ago and was a plaintiff-intervenor in *United States v. Boston* filed in July 2005. Yee recounted the following:

> When I first arrived in America, I wanted to learn [English], but I had no time. I had to work to survive. I had to work at a restaurant. All of us men had to work at the restaurants.

The women worked as seamstresses. We had to work 12-hour days. I am retired now, but back then, I would work all day. The restaurants were busy and there just was not enough staff to help out. I was lucky if I got out of work within 10 hours.

Like Mr. Yee, Byung Soo Park, another plaintiff in AALDEF's lawsuit against the New York City Board of Elections, understands the importance of learning English. Because of a demanding work schedule as a truck driver, however, Mr. Park cannot find the time to learn.

I became a citizen in October 2001 and registered to vote at the Korean American Voters' Council office with the help

New York ballots are listed in English, Spanish, and Chinese. Many minority voters prefer to vote using ballots in their native language.

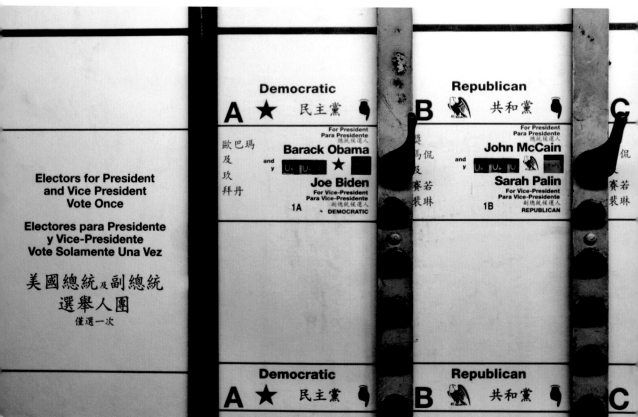

of their staff. Ever since I first registered to vote, I have never missed an election. Most recently, I voted in both Primary and General Elections, in September and November [2005]. Every time I vote I need to use the assistance of an interpreter. I need to continue voting with an interpreter because I am old. Many senior[s] . . . are limited English proficient, so we need interpreters in order to vote.

It also feels good to vote in America in my native language. Americans who know English should vote in English, but I did not go to school in the United States and I do not know English. I want to learn English but I have no time because I am a truck driver and work long hours on the road.

Korean Americans should be treated as United States citizens because that is what we are. I want us all to be treated equally.

For Mr. Yee, Mr. Park, and countless other new citizens, economic barriers have hindered their ability to learn English. Nevertheless, Mr. Yee, a visible community advocate for affordable housing in Boston's Chinatown, and co-chair of the Chinatown Resident Association, understands the importance of civic participation, voting, and language assistance. Without language assistance, Mr. Yee's ability to vote on civic matters that directly affect his community would be severely limited.

These voters embody what Congress had intended when it enacted Section 203 in 1975: "[T]he purpose of suspending English-only and requiring bilingual elections is not to correct the deficiencies of prior educational inequality. It is to permit persons disabled by such disparities to vote now."

The Use of Language Assistance

Language assistance removes barriers for LEP and first-time voters to register and cast informed votes. As AALDEF's recent multilingual exit poll surveys reveal, a large percentage of first-time voters use language assistance, in the form of either an interpreter or translated materials.

Asian American voters in general, including those who have voted in prior elections, have also expressed a consistent need for language assistance. In 2004 in Manhattan, of the 56 percent of Chinese American voters who were LEP, 34 percent were first-time voters, 41 percent said they needed an interpreter, and 39 percent said they needed translated materials to vote. In Queens County, of the 67 percent of Korean American voters who were LEP, 35 percent were first-time voters, 34 percent said they needed an interpreter, and 49 percent said they needed translated materials to vote.

Similarly, in Massachusetts, high LEP rates among the Chinese and Vietnamese communities in Boston and Dorchester encouraged the Justice Department's lawsuit against the City of Boston. In 2004 Dorchester's Vietnamese community was 74 percent LEP. Forty-five percent were first-time voters, 60 percent said they needed an interpreter, and 54 percent said they needed translated materials to vote. Among Boston's Chinese American community, where the LEP rate was 65 percent, 31 percent were first-time voters, 42 percent said they needed an interpreter, and 50 percent said they needed translated materials to vote.

Voter Registration Increases with Language Assistance

In San Diego County, voter registration increased 20 percent among Latinos and Filipinos after the Justice Department sued the county and later negotiated an agreement to enforce Section 203 requirements. Likewise, Vietnamese voter registration rose 40 percent after the county agreed to voluntarily provide language assistance for the Vietnamese American community. Similarly, in Harris County, Texas, Vietnamese American voters doubled their turnout in 2003 after the Justice Department enforced language assistance on the county's electronic voting machines. In the 2004 Elections, Harris County voters elected the first Vietnamese American to the state legislature.

The introduction of language assistance in jurisdictions where the Justice Department has pursued action shows a positive correlation between voter registration and turnout in LEP commu-

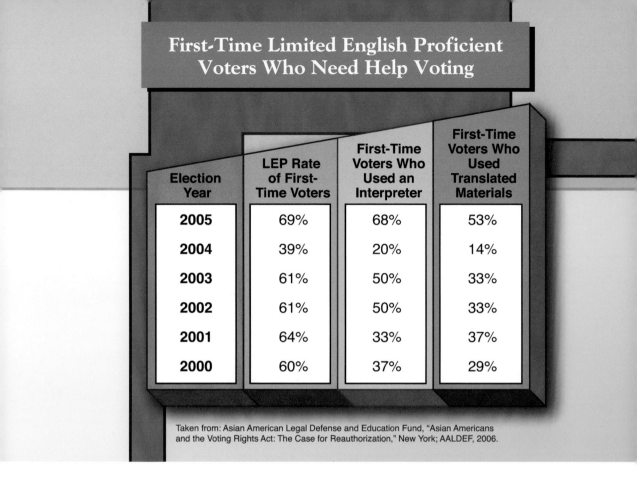

First-Time Limited English Proficient Voters Who Need Help Voting

Election Year	LEP Rate of First-Time Voters	First-Time Voters Who Used an Interpreter	First-Time Voters Who Used Translated Materials
2005	69%	68%	53%
2004	39%	20%	14%
2003	61%	50%	33%
2002	61%	50%	33%
2001	64%	33%	37%
2000	60%	37%	29%

Taken from: Asian American Legal Defense and Education Fund, "Asian Americans and the Voting Rights Act: The Case for Reauthorization," New York; AALDEF, 2006.

nities. As a result, the participation rates of Asian Americans nationally have increased dramatically over the last decade. While numerically registration and voting has steadily risen across all racial groups, Asian Americans are becoming active and civically engaged at an extremely fast pace. These growth rates are consistent with the eligible Asian electorate. The concentration of Asian citizens of voting age, has grown 73 percent from 1996 to 2004, compared to the national rate of 9 percent.

But absent reauthorization and expansion of Section 203, the progress that Asian American voters have made in terms of registration and turnout will stagnate or regress to pre-1992 levels.

Language Assistance and Asian American Elected Officials

The effectiveness of language assistance is further evident in the ability of Asian American candidates to win elected office oftentimes with overwhelming support from the Asian American community. Language assistance empowers Asian American voters and provides access to the elections process so they may register and elect their candidates of choice.

For example, in New York City, where Chinese American voters gained language assistance in 1992, the first Asian American, John Liu, was elected to the New York City Council in 2001. Statewide, Jimmy Meng was the first Asian American elected to the New York State Assembly in 2004. Both candidates relied heavily on support from voters in Flushing in Queens County, New York, where a large concentration of Asian American voters, many of whom are LEP, reside. Absent language assistance, Asian American candidates will have a harder time registering and turning out voters from the community, especially LEP voters who have difficulty navigating English ballots and voting materials. . . .

The Importance of Language Assistance

A recent ruling by a federal district court summarizes well the importance of language assistance:

> Voting without understanding the ballot is like attending a concert without being able to hear. Even if the voter, illiterate in English, may be able to distinguish one candidate's last name from another, the voter illiterate in English may not understand the office for which the various candidates are running, and surely cannot understand the various propositions, ranging from bond authorizations to constitutional amendments. But the meaningful right to vote extends beyond the immediate four corners of the voting machine. Advertisements of the location of polling places and sample official ballots are meaningless if a large segment of the voters in a particular precinct cannot read the material. Voting officials who cannot communicate with Spanish-speaking voters cannot discharge their duties. The voters themselves may have difficulty establishing their right to vote and to exercise their right to special assistance at the polling place.

THIRTEEN

English-Only Ballots Are Not Discriminatory

George Will

In the following viewpoint George Will, a syndicated columnist, writes that one of the requirements of becoming a U.S. citizen is the ability to read, write, and speak English. Allowing voters who have limited English proficiency to vote in another language proves that they have not met the requirements for American citizenship, the author argues. Will notes that voters who have limited English proficiency cannot understand the nation's political conversation, and voters who receive ballots in another language have no incentive to learn English.

"Of course not." That was Attorney General Alberto Gonzales's answer . . . on ABC's "This Week" [in 2007] when asked whether he would favor prohibiting bilingual ballots.

"Of course not"? Did he mean, "This is not something about which decent people differ"?

To understand why millions of conservatives do not trust Washington to think clearly or act reasonably about immigration, consider bilingual ballots. These conservatives, already worried that both the rule of law and national identity are becoming attenuated because of illegal immigration, now have another worry: The federal government's chief law enforcement official may need a refresher course on federal law pertaining to legal immigrants.

A Refresher on Federal Law

In 1906, the year before a rabbi in a Passover sermon coined the phrase "melting pot" during torrential immigration from Eastern and Southern Europe, Congress passed, and President Theodore

The controversy over English began in 1906 when President Theodore Roosevelt signed legislation requiring new immigrants to be proficient in speaking, writing, and reading English.

Roosevelt signed, legislation requiring people seeking to become naturalized citizens to demonstrate oral English fluency. In 1950 the requirement was strengthened to require people to "demonstrate an understanding of the English language, including an ability to read, write, and speak words in ordinary usage in the English language."

Hence, if someone needs a ballot written in a language other than English, that need proves the person obtained citizenship only because the law was not enforced when he or she sought citizenship. So one reason for ending ballots in languages other than English is that continuing them makes a mockery of the rule of law, including even the prospective McCain-Kennedy [the Secure America and Orderly Immigration] law that pro-immigration groups favor.

It contains several requirements that those aspiring to citizenship demonstrate "a knowledge of the English language" or "English fluency" in order "to promote the patriotic integration of prospective citizens into the American way of life" and into "American common values and traditions." How can legislators support language such as that and ballots in multiple languages?

Section 203

Fifty-six House Republicans have sent a letter, instigated by Rep. Steve King of Iowa, asking that Section 203 of the Voting Rights Act [providing language assistance to limited English proficient voters] be allowed to expire. When the measure was enacted in 1965, it said nothing about bilingual ballots. Section 203, requiring bilingual ballots in jurisdictions with certain demographic characteristics, was added in the 1975 extension of the act. The King letter was sent to Rep. James Sensenbrenner of Wisconsin, chairman of the House Judiciary Committee. He favors extending Section 203 and the rest of the act *until 2032* because it helps facilitate "the participation of language minority citizens in the political process."

But what public good is advanced by encouraging the participation of people who, by saying they require bilingual assistance, are saying they cannot understand the nation's political conversation? By receiving such assistance they are receiving a disincentive to become proficient in English.

Charges of Racism

It takes political bravery to propose pruning the Voting Rights Act, given the predictable charges of racism that are hurled so promiscuously nowadays. Senate Minority Leader Harry Reid, for example, has a liberal's reflex for discerning racism everywhere and for shouting "racist" as a substitute for argument. During Senate debate . . . on a measure to declare English the national language, he said: "While the intent may not be there, I really believe this amendment is racist."

Questions crowd upon one another. Was his opaque idea—well, perhaps it is not opaque to liberals—of *unintentional* racism merely a bow to Senate rules against personal slurs? What "race" does Reid think is being victimized? Are Spanish speakers members of a single race? Evidently Reid thinks something like that,

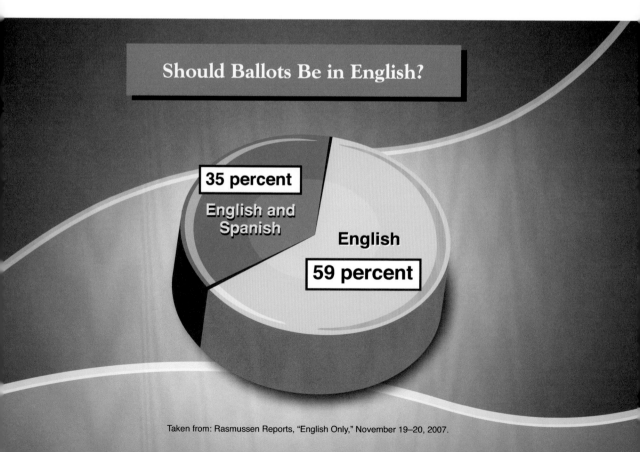

Should Ballots Be in English?

35 percent

English and Spanish

English

59 percent

Taken from: Rasmussen Reports, "English Only," November 19–20, 2007.

because his next sentence was: "I think it is directed basically to people who speak Spanish." Indeed, it is, but what has that to do with racism?

Declaring English the national language is a mere gesture. But by ending bilingual ballots, American law would perform its expressive function of buttressing, by codifying and vivifying, certain national assumptions and aspirations. Among those is this: The idea of citizenship becomes absurd when sundered from the ability to understand the nation's civic conversation.

What makes Americans generally welcoming of immigrants, and what makes immigrants generally assimilable, is that this is a creedal nation, one dedicated to certain propositions, not one whose origins and identity are bound up with ethnicity. But if you are to be welcomed to the enjoyment of American liberty, then America has a few expectations of you. One is that you can read the nation's founding documents and laws and can comprehend the political discourse that precedes the casting of ballots.

Is this unreasonable? Of course not.

FOURTEEN

The English Language Is Not Threatened in the United States

Dennis Baron

Dennis Baron, a professor of English and linguistics at the University of Illinois at Urbana, is the author of several books on English, including *The English-Only Question: An Official Language for Americans?* In the following viewpoint, taken from his blog the Web of Language, Baron examines the English Unity Act, a bill that would make English the official language of the United States. Baron contends that the bill is unnecessary, since America's laws have always been written, interpreted, and enforced in English. Furthermore, he asserts that it takes more than a common language to unify a nation; it takes our laws, customs, and spirit.

After centuries of welcoming the world's tired, poor, huddled masses to our shores, Americans are sending out a new message: "Speak English, or get out." In response to increases in immigration, both legal and otherwise, and to controversial translations of the national anthem and pledge of allegiance, 28 states and increasing numbers of cities across the U.S. are declaring English their official language. There's even a Pennsylvania sandwich shop where you can't order the famous Philly cheese steak unless you order it in English.

Dennis Baron, "The English Language Unity Act of 2007: It Takes More than a Language to Unify a Nation," The Web of Language, February 22, 2007. Reproduced by permission.

The English Unity Act

Anti-immigration forces are pushing for official English on the federal level as well. On Feb. 12 [2007], Rep. Steve King (R-Ia) reintroduced the "English Language Unity Act of 2007" (H.R. 997), a bill that has been kicking around in Congress for years, which would make English the official language of the United States. Bills like this arise from the fear that English, supposedly the glue holding a diverse and restless America together, is threatened by speakers of other languages.

Republican congressman Steve King of Iowa reintroduced the English Language Unity Act of 2007, which would make English the official language of the United States. Congress has debated the bill for years.

At first glance, the English [Language] Unity Act seems sensible. Declaring English official confirms what we already know: according to the 2000 Census, over 94% of Americans speak English. While the bill privileges English, it allows other languages to be used by the government to promote trade and tourism, protect public health and safety, preserve Native American languages, and teach foreign languages in school.

Unnecessary Protection

But Rep. King's bill also reveals the paranoia behind all official language legislation. It privileges the English versions of our laws because the bill's sponsors, who surely don't object to translating the Bible into English, insist that translating our laws, not to

Speaking and Understanding English in the United States Is Important

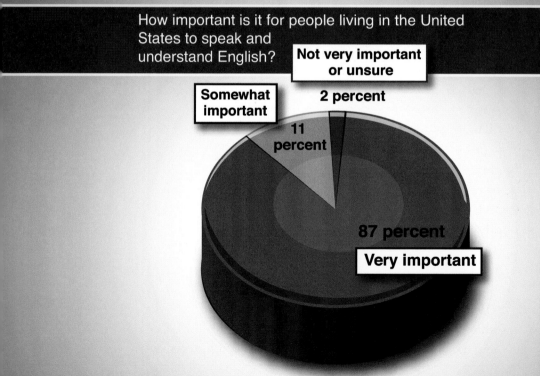

How important is it for people living in the United States to speak and understand English?

Not very important or unsure

Somewhat important

2 percent

11 percent

87 percent

Very important

Taken from: Rasmussen Reports, "English Only," November 19–20, 2007.

mention sacred secular texts like the Star-Spangled Banner and the Pledge of Allegiance, will distort or pervert their meaning. In any case such protection isn't necessary, because our laws have always been written, interpreted, and enforced in English.

The bill further requires that all citizens know enough English to read and understand America's Constitution and its laws, a requirement that seems unconstitutionally vague and ignores the fact that their meaning is regularly disputed by native English speakers who argue over it all the way to the Supreme Court.

Questionable Provisions

H.R. 997 contains one last questionable provision allowing anyone injured by a violation of the English Language Unity Act to sue for relief. Not only does this pave the way for nuisance suits, it's also not clear that anyone has ever met a government employee who refused to speak to them in English (most can't speak another language anyway).

The English Language Unity Act isn't an idealistic celebration of American unity, like the Fourth of July. It's actually aimed at Mexican immigrants, whose numbers Steve King is eager to reduce. In addition to mandating English, King actively supports an electrified fence across our border with Mexico (he demonstrated such a fence before the House of Representatives, and offered to build it himself), and he opposes the current practice of automatically granting citizenship to anyone born in the U.S.

When he was a state senator King wrote Iowa's official English law, which passed in 2002 amidst a panic that Spanish speakers were invading the state. It's true that the Census showed a doubling of Iowa's Spanish-speaking population between 1990 and 2000, from 1.5% to 2.9% of the total population. But that increase hardly constitutes an invading horde, and besides, most of Iowa's 80,000 Hispanics speak English as well as Spanish and pose no threat either to English or to national unity.

What Holds the Nation Together?

King introduced the English Language Unity Act on Abraham Lincoln's birthday because Lincoln brought a nation torn by

Civil War back together again, and King thinks that a nation threatened by Mexican immigration can be held together by a border fence and an official language. Many states in the former Confederacy don't celebrate Lincoln's birthday. Yet once they were brought back into the Union they stayed, because it takes more than a holiday to unify a nation. And as the British found out in 1776, and Lincoln found out in 1861, it takes more than a language, as well.

What holds the United States together isn't the English language but our laws, customs, traditions, and spirit. We don't need to add an official language to that mix because today's immigrants are already learning English as fast as they can, and making English official, whether it's at a restaurant counter or at the township, state, or federal level, sends immigrants a message even stronger than an electrified fence, that they're just not welcome here.

FIFTEEN

Teachers Should Help Preserve Their Students' Culture

Maria Franquiz and Carol Brochin-Ceballos

Maria Franquiz is associate professor in the Division of Bicultural Bilingual Studies at the University of Texas at San Antonio and a teacher consultant from the South Coast Writing Project. Carol Brochin-Ceballos is a teacher consultant from the South Texas Writing Project. In the following viewpoint the authors explain that teachers should incorporate their students' cultural background into their classrooms. Students' sense of belonging is constantly evolving, and by drawing on the students' cultures and beliefs, teachers can transform their classrooms into safe places to learn literacy and language development, the authors say. They argue that following four premises are useful for fostering cultural citizenship in the classroom: the use of culturally relevant books; the use of the students' culture as a resource for learning; encouraging students to speak and write about their cultures, values, and beliefs; and engaging in activities that have the potential to transform students.

One day in English I found out I got a 54. When I showed my mother she got mad and called my teacher, Mr. B. Then that night I saw Mr. B. But it was not him. He had long sharp teeth, long hair all over his boddy. I thought he was playing around, But he wasn't. It was for really. I siad, [sic]

Maria Franquiz and Carol Brochin-Ceballos, "Cultural Citizenship and Latino English Language Learners," *California English Journal*, Summer 2006. Reproduced by permission.

"How are you" But he did not answer. I siad again "How are you" But aggressively! Then he siad I've come for you because you failed. I was so scared I could not move or talk.
— (Rodrigo, 7th grader)

It was early November 2003 and Rodrigo's 7th grade language arts class was writing scary stories. These stories were to include action, dialogue and imagery. In Rodrigo's essay the action centered on a teacher becoming a werewolf who said, "I've come for you because you failed. . . ." Rodrigo responded, "'What are you talking about?' but he did not understand me." The essay continued, "I looked at my watch. It was 4:30. 4 hours before day break and I thought he could devour me before day break." The personification of a teacher as a werewolf was elaborated with details of sharp teeth, long hair, rough low tones, and sharp claws. The image of a teacher devouring his failing students ended with a sense of powerlessness because Rodrigo could not find a silver bullet needed to kill the werewolf. This is a powerful metaphor of Latino students' sense of powerlessness in the face of failing grades particularly in light of grisly statistics [as reported by Russell W. Rumberger and Gloria Rodriguez in their book, *Chicano Dropouts*] that indicate that "drop out rates for Latinos and Chicanos still remain almost four times as high as the rates for Whites."

As language arts educators observing Rodrigo in his class we were concerned that he was at risk for not completing middle school. In our experience, teachers who do not put Latina/o cultural citizenship at the center of their teaching would create a scary rather than a safe space for language and literacy development. By Latino cultural citizenship we are not referring to citizenship as defined in the social studies classroom but the right to use one's linguistic and cultural resources for learning. From this viewpoint classrooms are safe spaces where students' evolving sense of belonging to different communities is at the heart of curricula.

In this article we describe four premises for fostering cultural citizenship in classrooms. We developed these premises from the available research literature. Our goal is to describe each premise and provide classroom examples in which K–12 [kindergarten

These Latino student guitarists play Mexican songs in a jam session. Many people argue that teachers should help preserve their students' culture.

through grade twelve] teachers use these principles to guide their teaching of the language arts. Although we describe each premise separately we acknowledge that these four principles are dynamically interrelated.

The Four Premises of Latino Cultural Citizenship

1 - Providing Access to Culturally Relevant Texts

The premise of using culturally relevant texts is not new. Teachers who select culturally relevant texts take into account the necessity of providing literature that authentically represents students' cultural backgrounds. However, [Rosalinda] Barrera and [Ruth] Quiroa warn that some texts considered as culturally relevant actually promote cultural stereotypes. For example, Latinos in the classroom are often represented only as Mexican-Americans and/or as migrants. Thus, the premise of providing access to culturally relevant material takes into account a critical approach in selecting classroom literacy materials.

We observed an exemplary lesson in a fifth grade classroom with majority Mexican-American English language learners. These students had varying language and literacy skills. The teacher used the book, *Recordando mis Raices y Viviendo mis Tradiciones/Remembering my Roots and Living my Traditions* to elicit writing regarding the local traditions of their rural South Texas community. The story was written and illustrated by four Mexican-American young women. The students made direct personal connections with events in the story. They wrote amazing descriptive essays about quinceañeras (coming of age ceremonies), mariachi parties, carne asadas (barbeques), cascarones at Easter (confetti eggs), novíos pa' lazar (herding steer), among others. Because students were provided access to books written by authors, they were able to engage and produce culturally laden texts.

Using Cultural Assets

2 - Proposing Multiple Opportunities for Students to Use Their Cultural Assets

An assets orientation assumes that children from Latino homes do not necessarily come from a "culture of poverty." Rather, Latino children are invited to affirm and use their culture as a resource for learning. When teachers adopt an assets orientation, they provide multiple opportunities for students to use knowledge from their families and communities in the language arts classroom.

For example, in the case of a multi-age summer writing workshop, the teacher provided prompts to elicit drafts of memoirs, biographies, legends, poetry that were then used to create new drafts (storyboards), and finally used to create video poems. These poems were edited by the students and presented to members in their school and local community. Central to these opportunities was the invitation to develop their own unique voice through different literacy modalities.

In another example, Mrs. Z said she wanted to "create a sense of belonging." Towards this end she provided students with at least five prompts as choices for initiating writing during journal time in her language arts classroom. At least one of these prompts refers to making connections with family or community (e.g. things I do with my family or the wisdom of grandparents means . . .). A student, Teresa decided to write about the difficulty in communicating with her grandmother in Spanish because she no longer spoke her heritage language well. Her writing indicated that she was aware that not speaking Spanish had consequences at home. If she did not make personal effort to maintain her Spanish, she might not be able to understand her grandmother. For this reason, she recognized the value of developing her heritage language. Teresa was in a dilemma because bilingual instruction was not available to her. Through her writing this Mexican-American English language learner recognized the need for her heritage language rights and that she did not have access to them. By providing multiple prompts and repeated opportunities to write about her home culture, Mrs. Z created a venue for Teresa to explore her rights to cultural citizenship.

Cultural Preservation

3 - Fostering Cultural Preservation

In order to foster cultural preservation teachers ought to have an additive rather than subtractive approach toward unorthodox ways of producing writing about their ethnic community. They invite students to speak and write about their values and beliefs regarding texts and events in their personal lives.

An example to illustrate the preservation of community memories involves Rodrigo, the student who was haunted by his teacher as a werewolf. In an after-school educational setting, he brought a newspaper article to writing workshop about the recent demolition of a school in his local community. Rather than writing about his point of view he asked the teacher and students to visit the razed site where he produced an oral text with a microphone and video camera.

We're here in Cotulla in front of what used to be the old high school. . . . Before it was torn down there was a whole bunch of people here . . . trying to get in. They were former students who came here . . . they just wanted to get in to see their high school one last time. . . . They went to school here and what I think is that they want[ed] to have the memories of it . . . if they tore it down, they might forget the memories.

To support his claim that residents feared losing their memories Rodrigo decided to write interview questions to use with his Tia Rosie who, in earlier decades, had taught at the high school. This series of events re-engaged Rodrigo who appeared very constrained in the typical writing workshop format as well as in his seventh grade language arts classroom. His after-school teacher and peers validated his writing process by accepting the oral before the written text, the microphone before the pen. An inverted writing process affirmed his commitment to the cultural preservation of local historical memories. No longer scared of the werewolf, Rodrigo emerged as a powerful writer.

Agents of Change

4 - Engaging Students in Activities with Transformative Potential
When teachers engage students in activities with transformative potential they see their students as able to become agents of change. Toward this goal a safe space is created for students where they can link cultural practices from the home and community to broader struggles for social change. In these safe spaces students come to understand citizenship as cultural responsibility.

As an example of this principle we offer a story from a high school classroom. One student summarized the respect a teacher, Ms. White Chocolate (pseudonym provided by students), had earned in his class: "she understands the struggles of being brown in this school and in this town. She is white on the outside but brown on the inside." This teacher selected *Bless Me Ultima* to be read during English class. Arguments ensued during the reading of the book chapters. The Mexican and Chicano students argued about who is the real Mexican and if you have to speak Spanish to be Mexican? Messages about "English Only" in the media and local community made a strong impression on some students and they did not like the fact that the author, Rodolfo Anaya, used codeswitching [talking in both English and Spanish] in the book. Consequently, this literary strategy caused some students in the class to feel affirmed and connected, and others to feel estranged. In many ways the story provided a rich resource for examining group differences within the Mexican community and challenged the idea that students with common ethnic and socioeconomic backgrounds truly share common perceptions of the world. Because Ms. White Chocolate had created a safe space for literary discussion, students could talk about the tensions

Number of English Language Learners Climbs Dramatically

The total kindergarten through twelfth-grade (K–12) enrollment in the United States grew 12 percent from 45,443,389 in 1993–1994 to 49,619,090 in 2003–2004. In contrast, LEP enrollment increased by 65 percent from 3,037,922 students to 5,013,539 during the same time period.

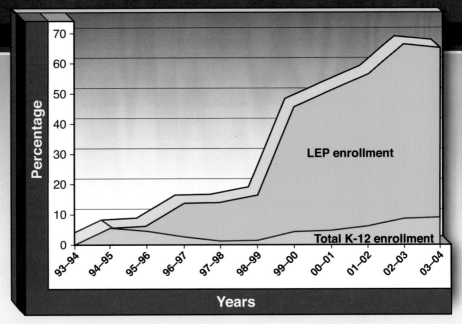

Taken from: Migration Information Source, "Spotlight on Limited English Proficient Students in the United States," February 2006.

accompanying their personal and collective ethnic identity. Her stance to use culturally relevant texts played an important role in helping students acknowledge the possibility of constructing more permeable boundaries between languages that are in direct contact in school and in the world beyond school. In this way she assisted students in disrupting beliefs about language. Over time these disruptions posed new possibilities and assisted students to seriously consider new ways of thinking. These types of engagements with contradictions, disruptions, and tensions have transformative potential and bear cultural responsibility.

Guided by these four principles we make the following recommendations in order to improve learning for Latino students in general and English language learners in particular. Educators interested in revising cultural relations with their students can:

- select culturally relevant texts that assist students to respond by establishing confidence in their cultural authority as writers.
- plan for literacy activities that support individual student's traditional as well as unorthodox processes as writers.
- provide students with choices to explore their linguistic and cultural heritage in literacy events.
- work collaboratively with students, parents, other teachers, and after-school programs to provide a broad range of opportunities for the affirmation and development of cultural citizenship.

Future research regarding effective literacy for Latino students can benefit by considering ways that cultural citizenship is visible or invisible in students' written products. We propose that educators make every effort to make claims for and questions of cultural citizenship visible in the literate lives of children living within and among the many linguistic and cultural borderlands of the twenty first century.

SIXTEEN

Adolescent Immigrants Have a Difficult Time Assimilating

Kristin Collins

Kristin Collins is a reporter for *The Raleigh (NC) News & Observer*. In the following viewpoint Collins explains that adolescent immigrants often have a difficult time finding their place in a society that resists accepting them. As a result some immigrant teens turn to gangs or self-destructive and criminal behavior in their attempt to find acceptance. Dropout and pregnancy rates for Hispanic teens are higher than for any other group. When their parents cannot speak English, Collins says, the children can avoid being accountable to their parents for their troublemaking. Ignoring the problems of adolescent immigrants will only make the problems worse as the teens grow into young adults and become increasingly alienated from society, she argues.

The debate over immigration often dwells on keeping illegal immigrants from slipping into the country, but when it comes to Hispanic youths who are already here, an opposite concern arises—too many are slipping away.

Hispanic youths, some born here, some who entered the country illegally but are growing up here, are at increasing risk of drifting into self-destructive and criminal behavior as they try to find their place in a culture that is at turns ambivalent and resistant about accepting them, according to those who have studied trends among Hispanic immigrants.

Bad News for Immigrant Teens

In North Carolina, a host of indicators show that many immigrant teens are not succeeding:

- Dropout rates for Hispanic students are higher than for any other group in the state. In the 2005–06 school year, nearly 9 percent of Hispanic high school students dropped out, compared with less than 4.5 percent of white students.
- More than half of North Carolina's Hispanic girls are expected to be pregnant before their 20th birthdays.
- A recent study of nearly 300 Hispanic immigrant teens in North Carolina, done by the UNC–Chapel Hill School of Social Work, sketched a picture of a population with emotional scars, uneducated parents and the pervasive feeling that they are not accepted by Americans.

More than half said they felt unsafe during their journeys to the United States, and a third said they were robbed, attacked, injured or became sick during the trip. Once here, more than 40 percent said they had faced ethnic discrimination, most frequently by their classmates.

Sixty-five percent of the teens agreed that "Americans generally feel superior to foreigners." Only 5 percent said they received any counseling.

Tracking Immigrant Teens

A national survey, run by New York University professor Marcelo Suárez-Orozco, tracked immigrant teens for five years. At the end, half were doing worse in school than when the study began. More than half of Hispanic children don't graduate in four years, Suárez-Orozco said.

The times hold both high promise and deep peril for immigrant children, he said.

"These kids are more likely than ever before in the history of the United States to go to Harvard University. And they're also

Fifteen percent of Hispanic American students between the ages of sixteen and nineteen drop out before finishing high school.

more likely to get involved in gangs and be involved in the criminal justice system," Suarez-Orozco said.

Juana Martinez, 17, a senior at Wake Forest-Rolesville [North Carolina] High School, is the president of the club Latinos Constructing a Better Future, formed as part of a gang prevention effort. At a recent meeting, she said, several boys talked about taunts from classmates.

"They said that some people have told them, 'Hey, go back to Mexico,'" Martinez said. "And some of them aren't even from Mexico. They were born here."

Martinez said she has watched many of her Hispanic class-mates drift into trouble: girls getting pregnant, boys wearing gang colors and forming segregated groups, others dropping out to take low-wage jobs.

Some Hispanic boys at her school, she said, feel that a grade point average higher than 2.5 is "too smart."

Clear Generational Differences in Latino Students' Post–High School Goals

Few students surveyed had large numbers of friends who dropped out of high school without graduating. However, there are clear generational differences regarding friends' plans to attend a four-year college. Over half of the third-generation students reported that many or most of their friends had such plans. Yet only 23 percent of second-generation and 16 percent of first-generation students felt the same.

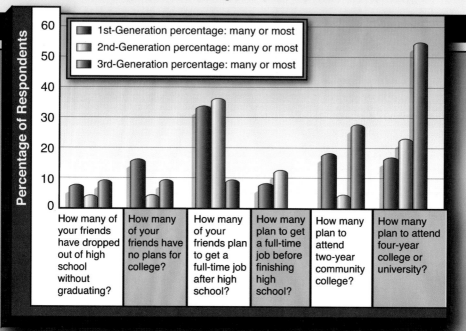

Taken from: Educational Attainment in Nebraska Survey, 2004 and 2005, Office of Latino/Latin American Studies, University of Nebraska at Omaha.

Troubled Family Circumstances

For many Hispanic students, their problems stem from their family circumstances. Their parents are often desperately poor and uneducated, and they come to the United States ill-equipped to deal with the pressure their children will face. Many work long hours and understand little of what goes on inside their children's schools.

Martinez, who moved to North Carolina from Mexico with her mother when she was 9, says her mother doesn't speak English. Her mother was never able to help with homework and felt uncomfortable visiting her schools. The elder Martinez didn't even know to ask for a report card, her daughter said.

Martinez pushed her mother to attend open houses and school meetings, where Martinez translated. But many other students don't make the effort.

Instead, they skip school and then delete the answering machine messages reporting their truancy—messages their parents don't understand.

Martinez spends two afternoons a week working with Hispanic students at Wake Forest Elementary School, hoping to give them the support she never had. For one boy who didn't know his letters, she wrote out their sounds in Spanish, hoping that his mother would work with him.

"He came back and said his mom told him she's sorry, but she didn't have time because she had to work," Martinez said.

Gangs Growing Fast

The price of ignoring the problems of immigrant Hispanic youth is that some become a problem for society at large.

A 2005 study showed that Hispanic gangs were the fastest-growing segment of North Carolina's mounting gang problem, accounting for about a quarter of the state's nearly 400 gangs. Many carry the names of notorious groups such as the Latin Kings or MS-13 that originated in California, Mexico and elsewhere.

Those who study gangs, however, say the threat doesn't come from afar.

Instead, research shows, many of North Carolina's gang members are homegrown—youths who felt isolated by language barriers or poverty, who were bullied and scorned by classmates, and who looked to a gang for acceptance. Much of North Carolina's gang activity can be traced to children and teens running in disorganized packs and claiming false ties to notorious international gangs, gang experts say.

A big myth about gangs "is that they are migrating across the country," said Buddy Howell, a researcher with the National Youth Gang Center, a U.S. Justice Department program. "Whenever you study an area with a gang problem, you find that most all of the gang members grew up there."

Like the waves of immigrants before them—Eastern Europeans, Italians, Irish—Hispanic youths are banding together in the face of a foreign environment, according to researchers, educators and social workers. As anger rises over a wave of Hispanic immigration, some say they fear that more Hispanic children will become alienated and turn to gangs.

Robbery Arrest

In the Triangle [Raleigh-Durham-Chapel Hill, North Carolina], the recent arrest of Nelson Rafael Hernandez put a face on the Hispanic gang problem. Hernandez, the oldest of four teens accused of robbing a Raleigh man and trying to rob a Durham woman, sneered and flashed gang signals as he stood in a Durham courtroom earlier this month [November 2007]. One of the teens police said was with Hernandez, a 16-year-old, was killed when, police said, he waved a gun at an officer outside a public library.

The mother of one suspect, another 16-year-old who lives in Durham, said that he had been expelled from school and that she was unable to stop him from running with the wrong crowd. She didn't know whether he had any true ties to the Latin Kings, the Chicago-based Hispanic gang that investigators say the teens were involved in.

Mike Figueras, who runs a gang prevention program for El Pueblo, a statewide Hispanic advocacy group, said children whose needs aren't met at home or at school are prime candidates for joining gangs.

They submit to beatings from fellow gang members, a common initiation ritual, and allow gang leaders to dictate their lives. He said most do it not for money, but for a feeling of belonging.

"It's so important to the kids that they're willing to do anything," Figueras said. "We're looking at 11-year-olds joining gangs."

Schools and advocates have started a host of programs designed to help immigrant children. Schools around the state offer English as a Second Language programs and employ Spanish-speaking Latino outreach workers. El Pueblo has started Hispanic clubs and leads anti-gang classes at schools across Wake County.

But William Lassiter, manager of the state's Center for the Prevention of School Violence, said that it's often difficult for educators to overcome all the obstacles facing Hispanic students. Some are four or five years behind and illiterate in their native language. Often, parents offer no information to help teachers, he said.

And if they join gangs, he said, educators often write them off.

"The big misconception is that these kids are not saveable," Lassiter said, "that once they're in, they're in for life. That's just not true. . . . We need to ask ourselves: How do we serve these kids better?"

What You Should Know About English Language Learners

Facts About English Language Learners

- According to the 2000 Census:
  - Eighty-two percent of people in the United States are native English speakers
  - There are 311 languages other than English spoken in the United States
  - Of these 311 languages, 162 languages are indigenous, and 149 are immigrant languages
- A 2003 study found that nearly 54 percent of English language learners in U.S. schools are immigrants.
- Nearly two-thirds of the country's Spanish speakers live in California, Texas, Florida, Illinois, New York, New Jersey, and Arizona.
- According to a 2006 report by the Pew Hispanic Center:
  - Only 23 percent of Latino immigrants are able to speak English very well
  - Eighty-eight percent of their adult, U.S.-born children speak English very well
  - Ninety-four percent of their children speak English very well
- A person is said to have limited English proficiency (LEP) if he or she speaks English "not well" or "not at all."
- A June 2008 survey found that 83 percent of Americans believe it is more important for immigrants to learn English than it is for Americans to become bilingual.

- English and Spanish are the most commonly spoken languages in the United States (82 percent and 10 percent, respectively). The next eight most commonly spoken languages in the United States (all 0.6 percent or lower) are French, Mandarin, German, Tagalog, Vietnamese, Italian, Korean, and Russian.
- Thirty states have passed laws or constitutional amendments making English their official language.
- Hawaii is officially bilingual, with English and Hawaiian being the two official languages of the state.
- In August 2000 President Bill Clinton signed an executive order mandating that federal agencies provide language assistance to people with limited English proficiency. Vital documents that must be translated include driver's license exams; ballots; cosmetology exams; application, consent and complaint forms; and prison rule books, among others.

What You Should Do About English Language Learners

Teachers, government employees, politicians, and even immigrants agree that the best way to succeed in the United States is to speak and read English. The question remains, however, over the best way to teach English language learners (ELLs). Should students be taught in bilingual education, where they are learning in both English and their primary language, or is English immersion—in which all lessons are in English—the best way to learn? What about those who are too old to go to school? How should they learn the English language? Classes that teach English as a second (or foreign) language (ESL) are popular and often fill up quickly. In addition some employers require that their employees speak English on the job. If an employee does not speak English, what are the options of the employer and the employee? And finally government regulations require that language assistance be provided for certain documents, such as voting ballots and various license applications and exams, to people who need it. What kind of assistance is required, and where can English language learners get it?

Deciding What Program Works Best

Because most English language learners are immigrants, the issue is closely tied to immigration, bilingual education, and official English/English-only policies, all of which are controversial and complex issues. How a school or business deals with ELLs can make the difference between success or failure in all aspects of a person's life.

First, if you are an English language learner in school, you must decide which program would work best for you. Do you think you would learn English better through bilingual education—in which some of your classes are taught in your primary language and some are taught in English—or through immersion programs, in which all your instruction, class work, discussion, and homework are done in English? There are advocates and detractors for both methods of teaching, and it is important to find someone who supports your decision. Ask your teachers, guidance counselor, or principal for assistance in getting the help you want and need. If the teachers or administrators at your school do not support your decision, perhaps there is another school you can attend. Many school districts have an open-enrollment policy in which students can attend the school of their choice. No matter which program you are in, if you are falling behind, do not be afraid to ask for additional help. Many schools offer tutoring programs for ELL students taught by their peers.

Adult English Language Learners

There are plenty of options available for adults who are English language learners. Libraries—both public and collegiate—offer a wealth of information. Many either have tutors who can help English language learners learn English or know where ELLs can get tutoring or take classes. Community colleges often offer classes in English as a second language (ESL), and some cities and towns offer ESL classes as well.

Laws Concerning the English Language

While the United States does not have a federal law mandating that English is the official language of the country, thirty states have passed such legislation. However, these laws are largely symbolic, since federal law trumps state law, and there are several provisions in federal law that require language assistance be made available to those who need it. Title VII of the 1964 Civil Rights Act protects against discrimination based on national origin. This act covers speaking English on the job as well as government documents that must be available in the locality's primary minority language. Section 203 of the 1975 Voting Rights Act requires that all information related to an election that is available in English must also be available in the primary minority language so that all citizens will have an effective opportunity to register, learn the details of the elections, and vote.

Executive Order 13166, signed by President Bill Clinton in August 2000, requires that all federal agencies provide "meaningful access" to its vital documents to people who have limited English proficiency (LEP). Vital documents include, for example, applications; consent and complaint forms; notices of rights and disciplinary action; notices advising LEP persons of the availability of free language assistance; prison rule books; written tests that do not assess English language competency, but rather competency for a particular license, job, or skill for which English competency is not required; and letters or notices that require a response from the beneficiary or client.

In many cases it is against the law for employers to require employees to speak English at all times while on the job. There are exceptions for jobs that involve public safety, such as police officers, firefighters, ambulance and emergency personnel, and the like. If an employer can prove a legitimate reason that employees must speak English on the job, that employer will be granted a legal exception. However, many courts have struck down such regulations, saying they are discriminatory and create a hostile work environment.

If You Have Been Discriminated Against

If you feel you have been discriminated against because of your national origin (a federally protected class), or because of your language skills (not specifically protected, but sometimes included under the protection of national origin), you have several options. First of all, you can try talking to the offending party and let him or her know of your concerns. In many cases simply informing people that their actions may be breaking the law may be enough to get them to stop. If asking someone to stop does not work, you can contact the Equal Employment Opportunity Commission (EEOC) or perhaps the American Civil Liberties Union (ACLU) to see if you have a valid case of discrimination. If one of these organizations chooses to represent you, it will do so at no cost to you. If the EEOC or the ACLU chooses not to take your case, they may give you other options, such as pursuing it with a lawyer at your own expense.

The editors have compiled the following list of organizations concerned with the issues debated in this book. The descriptions are derived from materials provided by the organizations. All have publications or information available for interested readers. The list was compiled on the date of publication of the present volume; the information provided here may change. Be aware that many organizations take several weeks or longer to respond to inquiries, so allow as much time as possible.

American Civil Liberties Union (ACLU)
125 Broad St., 18th Fl., New York, NY 10004
(212) 549-2500 • fax: (212) 549-2646
e-mail: aclu@aclu.org • Web site: www.aclu.org

The ACLU is a national organization that defends Americans' civil rights guaranteed in the U.S. Constitution. It adamantly opposes regulation of all forms of speech, including pornography and hate speech. The ACLU offers numerous reports, fact sheets, and policy statements on a wide variety of issues. Publications include the briefing papers "Backgrounder on English Only Policies in Congress" and "Voting Rights: About the VRA."

American Immigration Control Foundation (AICF)
222 West Main St., PO Box 525, Monterey, VA 24465
(540) 468-2022 • fax: (540) 468-2024
e-mail: aicfndn@ntelos.net • Web site: www.aicfoundation.com

The AICF believes the United States needs a reasonable immigration policy based on the nation's interests and capacity to assimilate newcomers. It is the country's largest publisher and distributor of pamphlets, monographs, and books about immigration, including history, law, culture, and demography. Its publications include the booklets *Erasing America—The Politics of a Borderless Nation, Selling our Birthright,* and *Public Costs of Immigration.*

American Library Association (ALA)
50 E. Huron St., Chicago, IL 60611
(800) 545-2433 • fax: (312) 440-9374
e-mail: ala@ala.org • Web site: www.ala.org

The ALA is the nation's primary professional organization for librarians. The ALA supports providing books and other library materials for all people in the community served by the library. It publishes the journal *American Libraries*.

Asian American Legal Defense and Education Foundation (AALDEF)
99 Hudson St., 12th Fl., New York, NY 10013
(212) 966-5932 • fax: (212) 966-4303
e-mail: info@aaldef.org • Web site: www.aaldef.org

AALDEF is a national organization that protects and promotes the civil rights of Asian Americans. AALDEF focuses on critical issues affecting Asian Americans, including immigrant rights, civic participation and voting rights, economic justice for workers, and language access to services. It publishes the report *Asian Americans and the Voting Rights Act: The Case for Reauthorization*.

Center for Equal Opportunity (CEO)
7700 Leesburg Pike, Ste. 231, Falls Church, VA 22043
(703) 442-0066 • fax: (703) 442-0449
Web site: www.ceousa.org

CEO is a conservative think tank dedicated to issues of race and ethnicity. It works to promote a color-blind society, in which race and skin color are no longer an issue. It therefore opposes bilingual education, because it segregates students by national origin, encourages identity politics, and fails to teach children English, which it believes is the single most important skill they can learn and the most important social glue holding the country together. Its Web site archives columns, congressional testimony, and editorials in various newspapers and magazines by staff members.

Center for Immigration Studies (CIS)
1522 K St. NW, Ste. 820, Washington, DC 20005-1202
(202) 466-8185 • fax: (202) 466-8076
e-mail: center@cis.org • Web site: www.cis.org

CIS is the nation's only think tank devoted exclusively to research and policy analysis of the economic, social, demographic, fiscal, and other impacts of immigration on the United States. It publishes backgrounds, papers, and other reports, including "Alingual Education," and maintains an archive of the reports and congressional testimony on its Web site.

English First
8001 Forbes Place, Ste. 102, Springfield, VA 22151
(703) 321-8818 fax: (703) 321-7636
e-mail: info@englishfirst.org • Web site: www.englishfirst.org

English First is a national grassroots lobbying organization whose goals are to make English the official language of the United States, give every child the chance to learn English, and eliminate costly multilingual policies. Its Web site provides resources and updates on U.S. government legislation concerning bilingual education.

Federation for American Immigration Reform (FAIR)
25 Massachusetts Ave. NW, Ste. 330, Washington, DC 20001
(202) 328-7004 • fax: (202) 387-3447
Web site: www.fairus.org

FAIR seeks to improve border security, stop illegal immigration, and reduce immigration levels from more than 1 million per year to more traditional rates of about three hundred thousand a year. The organization contends that the influx of immigrants—whose children often have limited English proficiency—is burdening public schools' finances and teachers. Its publications include *Limited English Proficiency Enrollment and Rapidly Rising Costs*, *Breaking the Piggy Bank: How Illegal Immigration Is Sending Schools Into the Red*, and *No Room to Learn: Immigration and School Overcrowding*.

Institute for Language and Education Policy
PO Box 5960, Takoma Park, MD 20913
e-mail: bilingualed@starpower.net
Web site: www.elladvocates.org

The institute was incorporated to educate the public on research-based strategies that promote academic excellence and equity for English and heritage language learners. The institute's members are teachers, administrators, professors, students, researchers, and others who believe that strong advocacy for students is essential. Toward that end, the institute issues briefs, policy analyses, news bulletins, commentary articles, online publications, media outreach, and public forums on issues including the No Child Left Behind Act, the English Only movement, and bilingual and heritage language education.

Mexican American Legal Defense and Education Foundation (MALDEF)
634 S. Spring St., 11th Fl., Los Angeles, CA 90014
(213) 629-2512
Web site: www.maldef.org

MALDEF is a national nonprofit organization whose mission is to protect and promote the civil rights of the more than 45 million Latinos living in the United States, primarily in the areas of employment, education, immigrants' rights, political access, and public resource equity. On its Web site are policy papers, congressional testimony, its quarterly newsletter *Maldef Newsletter*, and the the briefing book *Language Rights*.

National Association for Bilingual Education (NABE)
1313 L St. NW, Ste. 210, Washington, DC 20005
(202) 898-1829 fax: (202) 789-2866
Web site: www.nabe.org

The NABE is the only national professional organization devoted to representing bilingual learners and bilingual education professionals. NABE's mission is to advocate for bilingual and English language learners and their families. It also seeks to cultivate a multilingual, multicultural society by supporting and promoting policy, programs, and research that yield academic success, value native language, lead to English proficiency, and respect cultural and linguistic diversity. Its publications include *Language Learner Magazine* and *Bilingual Research Journal*.

National Council of La Raza (NCLR)

1126 Sixteenth St. NW, Washington, DC 20036
(202) 785-1670 • fax: (202) 776-1792
e-mail: comments@nclr.org • Web site: www.nclr.org

NCLR is the largest Latino civil rights and advocacy organization in the United States. It uses applied research, policy analysis, and advocacy to help the public understand Hispanic needs and to encourage the adoption of programs and policies that benefit Hispanics. Its publications include the documents *Hispanic Education in the United States*, *Educating English Language Learners*, and the fact sheet *Voting Technology for Language Minorities*.

People for the American Way (PFAW)

2000 M St. NW, Suite 400, Washington, DC 20036
(202) 467-4999 or (800) 326-PFAW • fax: (202) 293-2672
e-mail: pfaw@pfaw.org • Web site: www.pfaw.org

PFAW works to promote citizen participation in democracy and safeguard the principles of the U.S. Constitution, including language assistance to voters with limited English proficiency. It publishes a variety of fact sheets, articles, and position statements on its Web Site, such as "Renewal of the Voting Rights Act of 1965: What Are the Issues?" and distributes the e-mail newsletter *Freedom to Learn Online*.

ProEnglish

1601 N. Kent St., Ste. 1100, Arlington, VA 22209
(703) 816-8821 • fax: (571) 527-2813
e-mail: mail@proenglish.org • Web site: www.proenglish.org

ProEnglish supports the establishment of English as the official language of the United States. It cites public opinion and the court system to defend the role of the English language as the nation's common and unifying language. On its Web site it maintains articles, fact sheets, and backgrounders about official English, bilingual education, bilingual ballots, and English on the job.

Teachers of English to Speakers of Other Languages (TESOL)
700 S. Washington St., Ste. 200, Alexandria, VA 22314
(888) 547-3369 • fax: (703) 836-6447
e-mail: info@tesol.org • Web site: www.tesol.org

TESOL aims to strengthen effective instruction and learning of English while respecting individual rights. The organization provides information to students, schools, and professionals around the world who are involved in English as a second or foreign language and promotes research and teacher certification. Among the information available on its Web site are magazines and books on how to teach English as a second language.

U.S. Department of Education Office of English Language Acquisition (OELA)
U.S. Department of Education, 400 Maryland Ave. SW
Washington, DC 20202
(800) 872-5327 or (202) 401-1576
Web site: www.ed.gov/about/offices/list/oela/index.html

OELA's mission is to identify major issues affecting the education of English language learners (ELLs) and to provide national leadership to help ensure that ELLs and immigrant students attain English proficiency and achieve academically. OELA administers programs and activities associated with the No Child Left Behind Act. Among the publications available on its Web site is the report *Language of Opportunity* and the briefing *U.S. English Language Learner Students in U.S. Public Schools: 1994 and 2000.*

U.S. English Foundation
1747 Pennsylvania Ave. NW, Ste. 1050
Washington, DC 20006

(202) 833-0100 fax: (202) 833-0108
e-mail: info@usenglish.org • Web site: www.usenglish.org

The U.S. English Foundation, a separate organization from U.S. English Inc., disseminates information on English teaching methods, sponsors educational programs, develops English instructional materials, represents the interests of official English advocates before state and federal courts, and promotes opportunities for people living in the United States to learn English. On its Web site is a database of English as a second language classes across the country. Its publications include the briefings *Driver's License Nonsense*, *Avoiding an American Quebec*, and *English: The Global Language*.

U.S. English Inc.
1747 Pennsylvania Ave. NW, Ste. 1050
Washington, DC 20006
(202) 833-0100 • fax: (202) 833-0108
Web site: www.us-english.org

U.S. English Inc. is the country's largest citizens' action group dedicated to making English the official language of the United States. It believes that making English America's official language will expand opportunities for immigrants to learn and speak English, the single greatest empowering tool that immigrants must have to succeed. Its Web site maintains a database of legislation relating to official English and news about English-only lawsuits. U.S. English Inc. is a separate organization from the U.S. English Foundation.

BIBLIOGRAPHY

Books

James Crawford, *Advocating for English Learners: Selected Essays*. Buffalo, NY: Multilingual Matters, 2008.

Jim Cummins and Nancy H. Hornberger, eds., *Bilingual Education*. New York: Springer, 2008.

Carole Edelsky, *With Literacy and Justice for All: Rethinking the Social in Language and Education*. Mahwah, NJ: Lawrence Erlbaum, 2006.

Patricia Gándara and Frances Contreras, *The Latino Education Crisis: The Consequences of Failed Social Policies*. Cambridge, MA: Harvard University Press, 2009.

Ofelia Garcia and Colin Baker, eds., *Bilingual Education: An Introductory Reader*. Buffalo: Multilingual Matters, 2007.

Joshué M. González, ed., *Encyclopedia of Bilingual Education*. Thousand Oaks, CA: Sage, 2008.

Francois Grosjean, *Studying Bilinguals*. New York: Oxford University Press, 2008.

Caroline Hondo, Mary E. Gardiner, and Yolanda Sapien, *Latino Dropouts in Rural America: Realities and Possibilities*. Albany: State University of New York, 2008.

Barbara Zurer Pearson, *Raising a Bilingual Child*. New York: Living Language, 2008.

Otto Santa Ana, ed., *Tongue-Tied: The Lives of Multilingual Children in Public Education*. Lanham, MD: Rowman & Littlefield, 2004.

Tom Stritikus, *Immigrant Children and the Politics of English-Only: Views from the Classroom*. New York: LFB Scholarly, 2002.

Lucy Tse, *Why Don't They Learn English? Separating Fact from Fallacy in the U.S. Language Debate*. New York: Teachers College Press, 2001.

Periodicals

Tresa Baldas, "Workers Challenge English-Only Rules," *National Law Journal*, June 11, 2007.

Jim Boulet Jr., "The Salvation Army or the Hispanic Caucus?" *Human Events*, November 21, 2007.

Economist, "The English Patients," June 7, 2007.

Cathleen Flahardy, "Language Barriers," *Inside Counsel*, March 2008.

Kari Gibson, "English Only Court Cases Involving the U.S. Workplace: The Myths of Language Use and the Homogenization of Bilingual Workers' Identities," *Second Language Studies*, Spring 2004.

Austan Goolsbee, "Legislate Learning English? If Only It Were So Easy," *New York Times*, June 22, 2006.

Patricia Kilday Hart, "When Juan Can't Read," *Texas Monthly*, October 2006.

Kelley Holland, "When English Is the Rule at Work," *New York Times*, January 27, 2008.

Mike King, "How to Teach English," *Atlanta Journal-Constitution*, April 13, 2007.

Leonard Kniffel, "English Only Is English Lonely," *American Libraries*, November 2007.

Charles Krauthammer, "In Plain English: Let's Make It Official," *Time*, June 4, 2006.

Mauro E. Mujica, "English: Not America's Language?" *Globalist*, June 19, 2003.

National Review, "Speak Up in English," October 22, 2007.

Ruben Navarrette Jr., "Se Habla English," *Hispanic*, June 2006.

Jay Nordlinger, "Bassackwards: Construction Spanish and Other Signs of the Times," *National Review*, January 29, 2007.

Todd Douglas Quesada, "Spanish Spoken Here," *American Libraries*, November 2007.

Michael Reagan, "Speak English, Get Ahead," *Human Events*, November 23, 2007.

Julia Stephens, "English Spoken Here," *American Libraries*, November 2007.

INDEX

National Center for
Education Statistics, 59
National Institute for
Occupational Safety and
Health, 45
Navarette, Ruben, 88
New York Times (newspaper),
41
Nichols, Lau v. (1974), 36
No Child Left Behind Act
(NCLB, 2001), 16, 17, 19,
36–37

O
Opinion polls. *See* Surveys
Ortiz, Freddy, 42

P
Park, Byung Soo, 94–95
Pelosi, Nancy, 86, 87, 90
Perez, Eddie, 41–42
Pew Research Center, 39–40
Polls. *See* Surveys
President's National Security
Language Initiative, 56
Proficiency standards, 25

Q
Quiroa, Ruth, 111

R
Race Project (Web site), 80
Reid, Harry, 102
Rethinking Schools (magazine),
12, 13
Rodriguez, Gloria, 110
Rodriguez, Liza, 59

Roosevelt, Theodore,
100–101
Rosas, Andres, 63
Rumberger, Russell W., 110

S
Salas, Kelley Dawson, 12
Salvation Army, 80, 83, 84
EEOC litigation against,
88–89
Samano, Jose Martin, 90
Schwarzenegger, Arnold, 88
Sensenbrenner, James, 101
States
English as official language
and, 14–15, 46
Suárez-Orozco, Marcelo,
118–119
Surveys
immigrants learning English,
71
on driver's license exams
in English, *76*
on English-only ballots,
102
on English-only workplace
policies, *87*

T
Torres, Arnoldo, 41
Trasviña, John, 75
Tucker, James Thomas, 70, 72

U
United States
English should be official
language of, 39–48

English-speaking ability of
   residents of, 52, 53
government assistance to
   immigrants and, 71
spending on English lan-
   guage education by, 59,
   60
United States v. Boston (2005),
   93, 96
Urban Institute, 20
U.S. English Foundation, 64
Uyehara, Paul, 62

V
Views of a Changing World
   (Pew Research Center
   survey), 39–40
Voters,
   first-time, 97

importance of language
   assistance to, 98
Voting Rights Act, 102
   Section 203, 95

W
The Waiting List Myth (U.S.
   English Foundation), 64
Will, George, 99
Workplace
   English-only policies are
      discriminatory, 80–85
   English-only policies help
      workers assimilate, 86–91
   support for English-only
      policies in, 87

Y
Yee, Henry, 93–94, 95